Observations & Reflections
On Texas Folklore

Edited & with Photographs by

Francis Edward Abernethy

Line Drawings by
James R. Snyder

University of North Texas Press
Denton, Texas

A PREFACE

(In which the editor presents his credentials, among other things)

I KNOW how you feel. I felt the same way when I first heard that the headquarters for the Texas Folklore Society was leaving Austin and The University of Texas campus. I could never imagine it anywhere else except at the place of the omphalos. Then the meeting was called to order, the motion was made, seconded, and passed, and the transfer was duly recorded in the minutes.

We moved during the burnt-out end of August, Wilson and I, in the midst of posting final grades, campus construction, and a quiet sadness. We sweated and cussed some as we packed the Society's materials in cardboard boxes and carried them out to the station wagon parked behind Parlin Hall. We took down the pictures of Lomax and Payne and Thompson and some Cisneros sketches that had been used in *The Healer of Los Olmos*. Frank Dobie's old felt hat with a turkey feather in the band was sitting on a filing cabinet, so we put it in. Very gently we loaded a box of Mody's paisanos, five or six of them. Wilson had deposited much of the early correspondence in the State Archives, but several boxes of old programs, advertisements, letters, and brochures remained as relics of our ancestors and of our beginnings. And there were the Society's publications, more than thirty of them that stretched back to Stith Thompson's Volume I in 1916. These make up our umbilicus, the visible chain of the Society's being, that makes us all a part of it from its inception in 1909.

The Texas Folklore Society is now headquartered on the Stephen F. Austin State University campus in Nacogdoches. I have hung the pictures, shelved our volumes, and filed the materials of our business. Our offices are in the basement of one of the campus' original buildings. Our quarters aren't new and shiny, but then neither are we. The building, named after Thomas J. Rusk, is appropriately solid and comfortable, and the campus is located on the old Rusk homestead. The pines reach tall to the sky here, and their roots grow deep in the red dirt. This part of the country has been Texas for a long time, and its history and traditions form a fitting setting for the Society's headquarters.

As the new man on the job, I guess I ought to present some credentials. Although I was born in Oklahoma, that area was Greer County, Texas, when my grandparents settled there. Since those first few months as an Okie I've lived in the Panhandle dust and the Gulf Coastal swamps, five miles from the nearest mailbox and in the middle of Big D. I began to consciously think Texas during the centennial year of '36, and thereafter my education was liberally seasoned with my own Texas Trinity—Dobie, Boatright, and Bedicheck.

I shall do my best to keep the lid on my Texas chauvinism, but I am foolish about this state. It has blessed me bountifully in spirit and in store and I love it, head to toe, fingertip to fingertip. When you are in love with someone and you are really interested in her and not in your own reflection in her eyes, you are fascinated by every round inch of her, past and present. I feel that way about Texas and studying her folklore is getting to know her more delicately and more intimately.

This does not mean that I view folklore as an exercise in regionalism or provincialism. I do not. Nor do I view it as a snug nest to curl up in to retreat from the cold, sharp edges of the present. To me folklore is the ultimate, all-encompassing field of study. I see a decade, a millennium or an age go by, but the creature man remains the same, activated by the same urges, responding in the same way as did his ancient cave-dwelling ancestors. Only the symbols change. The gods shift their shape but continue to answer to the same needs, and folklore is the demonstration of this eternal kinship. A single seed contains the essence of all life, and the Texas and

Southwestern folklore in this volume contains the essence of universal phenomena. The time and the place and the people happened in Texas, but the hunters and fighters and singers of songs are universals, representatives of the repetitions of history and the everlasting oneness of man.

A major concern of mine in Texas folklore has been stimulated by my association with the Institute of Texan Cultures. A tour of its quarters in San Antonio reminds us that we have the whole world in our borders, every ethnic distinction and every color, from blue-eyed Nordic to black-eyed Bantu. The phenomenon of folklore can be studied and enjoyed here in all its ramifications and derivations. I can envision a future TFS annual that is devoted to a survey and sampling of the folklore of the many different ethnic cultures in Texas, but we are going to have to fill some gaps. Our annuals are full of Mexican folklore, but there is remarkably little Negro folklore and even less Cajun lore. I had a student once who brought in Czech folklore, and another one from Brenham or thereabouts who talked a lot of German folklore but never got any down on paper. And as scarce as Indians are generally, there are still enough within our borders to talk to them about their own particular ways of life. We have an untapped treasure in the Southwest, but we are going to have to get to scratching if we ever hope to share it.

Editing this volume has been a pleasure. I have gotten together many of my favorites among Texas folklorists, and I have enjoyed visiting with them again. They are all my close friends and I hope you realize how much restraint was required on my part to keep from telling how great they all are as writers and as personalities. I am subjective about these people so if there is some article here that you don't like, don't tell me about it.

I wish to thank Dr. Ralph W. Steen, the president of Stephen F. Austin State University, for his encouragement and assistance in getting the Society functioning on this campus; Dr. Roy E. Cain, the head of the English Department, for his generosity and support; and Mrs. Martha Dickson, the Society's secretary, for keeping our house—and this edition—in excellent and understandable order. And as always, I thank Hazel.

Observations and Reflections is dedicated to Wilson M. Hudson, Jr., former Secretary-Editor (1964-1971) and Fellow of the Texas Folklore Society. To him I owe the most.

FRANCIS EDWARD ABERNETHY
Nacogdoches, Texas
April 18, 1972

CONTENTS

OBSERVATIONS & REFLECTIONS ON TEXAS FOLKLORE

OBSERVATIONS & REFLECTIONS
OF A DEER HUNTER

J. Frank Dobie (edited by Bertha McKee Dobie)

WHEN a person stands or sits in the quietness of the country, especially in a brush pasture, he hears sounds that he would hardly detect if he were moving. His immobility makes the creatures unaware of him. The flip of a mockingbird's wing near him may make him suspect for an instant that a buck deer is nearing his stand; the rustle of an armadillo in leaves will sound monstrously loud; the stepping of a cow or her biting off grass a hundred yards away will fill his ears; a woodrat's sudden movement or gnawing about his nest of sticks and dried prickly pear leaves will make him suspicious. Many little, only momentary, unidentifiable sounds break the silence.

If this silent, motionless listener and watcher is a deer hunter he reflects on how much noise his clumsy body must make to listening animals as he passes through brush, over brittle grass, clods and rocks. A rusty lizard on the bark of a tree may make a startling noise to a man in the tree listening and looking for a deer to come within range. Unless wind and terrain are very favorable, he can hardly hope to stalk an always listening deer. He may walk for hours over thick sign without seeing even a doe. The deer have heard him and slipped away, unseen and unheard, in the brush. Among the thousands of hunters who go out for deer in Texas before the rutting season is on, comparatively few are sufficiently light footed, supple and noiseless to bring in venison by stalking.

3

Of course, after bucks get doe on their consciousness they are helpless. Sometimes a sex-possessed buck will nearly run over a man.

When, about the first of December, 1955, I went as Will Caswell's guest to hunt on a big ranch in Webb County, up the Rio Grande from Laredo, the bucks were plenty self-possessed. One late afternoon Tad (W. V.) Brenizer, the ramrod of the hunting party, put a feather-light metal chair under a willow tree near a big tank of water, put a green quilt over the chair to camouflage it and me, and told me to sit until he returned at dark. The tree trunk at my back was very comfortable. I kicked away all the twigs about my feet so that I could move them without making the least noise. I don't recall ever having been so comfortable at a stand. My inclination is always to hunt deer instead of letting them hunt me, but now I was too comfortable to want to move—and too interested.

The first thing I heard was a big blue heron—often miscalled crane—fishing in the tank. This heron does not care how much noise he makes, and he makes plenty with both wings and mouth. Some cows that had watered grazed up near me, and then I saw my first deer—a doe and a last spring's fawn. They came from where I expected them to come, out of a prickly pear thicket, and crawled under a barbed wire fence of four strands instead of jumping over it. They came through the grazing cows right out in front of me and then turned to drink from a brush-lined gully into which tank water was backed. I could not see them drinking on account of the brush, but saw a half-Brahman cow looking at them very intently. I was afraid they would pass on around me and smell me, but they came back to nibble on fresh growth in the low, moist ground between me and the tank basin. They passed within thirty feet of me, the doe dunnish in color, the fawn blue-black in its fat. I think the doe had sniffed a suspicious scent while drinking, for she was against lingering and soon bounded away, the fawn following.

Now for a while the only stir of life to engage my attention was from birds. At this time of year flickers and golden-fronted woodpeckers from the north are abundant in many parts of southern Texas. Several seemed to be holding a convention about my tank, where there are many dead trees. Their bold cries and energetic peckings into the dead trees cheered me up. I am sure that the natural noises of birds and other animals about a spot of ground make deer less suspicious of enemies at it.

Two belted kingfishers were fishing from dead trees in the water. Each would remain silent and stationary for a while and then with rattling cry fly across the water for another perch. I saw two unsuccessful dives after fish. At the same time that the big kingfishers were looking for waterlife, a pair of vermilion flycatchers brightened the air by darting after insects from twigs of the dead bushes in the water.

A killdee had its station at the edge of the water about seventy-five feet from me. The proper name is killdeer, but I grew up calling the bird killdee; the name is taken from its cry, and it seems to me to say "killdee" rather than "killdeer." The Mexicans call it "tildee." As I watched this one and occasionally heard others, I remembered what my friend Santos Cortez once told me. Santos was a good hunter. He said that one morning before daylight while he was moving down a watered glade as slow as a snail he heard killdees cry out a short distance away, not startled by him, and straining his eyes, saw the horns of seven big bucks, following each other. He could hardly make out their bodies against the ground but their horns were visible against the sky. Their coming had caused the ground-roosting killdees to fly and, as always when they rise, to cry out.

And now one of the biggest coyotes I have ever seen came to drink. I did not see his approach but heard his careless step into the edge of the water and detected his lapping. He took longer to drink than the doe and the fawn had taken, and then came into and kept in view as he trotted around the tank.

I looked across the tank and saw a grown deer standing on the top of the dam in an open spot between mesquites. The sun was down and in the dimming light I had to use my binoculars to make sure whether this deer, about three hundred yards away, had horns or not. It had no horns. The doe did not see me but kept looking behind and to one side of her. I held the binoculars up watching her until my arms tired. She came down the dam as if to drink but did not drink. She got behind a sprangly mesquite near the water border and stood there. I had to use the binoculars again, raised slowly, slowly, for I was in full view of her, to locate her head.

And now I saw a deer under a willow tree, near the edge of the water, between me and the mesquite-hidden doe. It also was horn-less, a doe. She began coming toward me, now and then nipping a bite of vegetation. When within about forty yards she gave a start-led look and there I saw two fawns—called "yearlings," though they will not be a year old until May or June. All three came where the first doe and fawn had come. I could have counted the hairs in the eyebrows of one of them, or roped it had I had a rope and been a little faster than greased lightning. One of them went to wading in shallow water, nipping tops from a kind of weed. I could hear the light splashes of feet in the water and mud.

Now it was growing too dark to make out any object more than a few yards away. I heard the jeep coming and the deer heard a man get out of it to come to me. They were gone. I had had a won-derful evening's hunt—and what good company! I had not seen a buck but I had been expecting for two hours and had been enter-tained beyond expectation the whole time.

Yet being entertained by sidelines can cost a hunter his deer. The biggest buck I ever saw I missed because I was not single-minded in purpose as any expert hunter should be. It was on a high hill of black chaparral in La Salle County overlooking a vast country in-cluding wide sacahuiste flats along the Nueces River. What a fine place for a Comanche or Lipan sentinel, I thought, and for a signal smoke. I went scouting about for the site of a fire. I had found a rough circle of smoked rocks and was searching the ground for arrowheads when I looked up and saw a mighty-antlered buck, almost black, his hips as wide as a Spanish mule's. He was looking at me when I raised up, and in a second he was out of sight.

The first thing that took me away from the world after I started out on a recent hunt was a vast congregation of blackbirds in the Comal valley near New Braunfels. They were not all in one flock. There were several flocks, some flying, some alighting. I stopped my car to one side of the road and got out to watch them. I esti-mated that there might be a mile long flight of the blackbirds, all taken together, and that the width of the flights might average fifty feet. There seemed to be one bird to the square foot in the dark masses. If so, 50 times 5280 feet would make 264,000 blackbirds—more than a quarter of a million. As one old frontiersman said to another who was praying aloud in a meeting, during a great drouth, for "barrels of flour, barrels of sugar, barrels of bacon, barrels of beans," and then "barrels of pepper," "Hell that's too much pepper." But there certainly were tens of thousands of blackbirds.

I was to hunt on Edgar Kincaid, Sr.'s Pablo Ranch out from Eagle Pass. On this and on a very large ranch he leased in the same county, Maverick, I hunted deer for many seasons. The first morning of hunting, I saw what I took to be a buck about half a mile away on a hill. I got only one glimpse of him passing between bushes, browsing east. I veered, kept under cover, and moved towards a spot where I thought I might intercept him. I was a little too previous, and after I heard his snort, blamed myself and hunted down a prickly pear thicket mixed with brush. I came into a trail that gave me a view for about a hundred yards and decided to linger a bit. The morning was brisk, and I set a rat's den on fire in a clump of prickly pear.

The architecture of a rat's den in the brush country is a marvel. The big white-bellied wood rats make tunnels around the pear roots; over the tunnels and approaches out from them, all around the pear, they drag in and heap up sticks, thorns, dried pear leaves, cow chips, bones, rocks. I have seen mounds three or four feet high. These rats are meaty and juicy. They have many enemies, both by day and night—owls, hawks, badgers, coyotes, rattlesnakes, other snakes, wildcats. Generation after generation of the big rats occupying a nest adds to the barricade. In some of the larger nests, I am told, as many as twenty rats make their home. It is seldom, however, that one runs out while its house is on fire. Coyotes will come up to the ashes after man has gone and dig for rat meat, either fresh or roasted. Pear-burners scorching pines off the pear so that cattle can eat the pads continually set rat nests on fire, and coyotes learn to follow the pear burners for the rats.

Bobcats also probably learn that fire in a prickly pear country means rat meat. Anyhow, not long after I had set the rat nest to burning, I heard, while standing and looking, a very slight noise in the brush, and out popped a big wildcat. He saw me motionless, and stopped dead still, gazing through me. He was not more than twelve feet away. For maybe two minutes neither of us moved or batted an eye. Then, in a second, he was back in cover and out of sight. Had I killed my buck, I should never have met him. I wanted that buck, but all things considered, I am glad I missed him and met the wildcat.

I should not have set the rat nest afire perhaps had I not had another experience with flame and smoke. One drizzly winter day several years ago while deer-hunting in Uvalde County, I stopped for noon under a big live oak. There was some fairly dry wood under it and I wanted to dry my feet; so I made a small fire. It smoked heavily, and presently I saw two yearling deer coming up to investigate. I froze still on the ground, against the oak. They came within a few yards, looked, smelled, stamped their sharp little hooves out of impatience at not understanding what had excited their curiosity, and stayed about until I was tired of not moving. I remember them much more vividly and with much more pleasure than I remember the buck killed that afternoon.

On the second morning of my hunt I killed a very fat young javelina sow, the meat of which proved to be as good as the proverbial "venison and honey." In the late afternoon I was slowly walking through brush and prickly pear when six startled javelinas startled me. There was a sow with a single pig; the other four were grown. All but one ran off. He wanted to see what the intruder was. I did not move. He finally decided to investigate; he made about a two-thirds circle of me and then retraced that circular route two times, keeping not more than fifty steps away. Then one of the peccaries that had run off appeared and made the same sort of semi-circular tour. Presently this animal was joined by two others, one of them a big boar. They advanced cautiously to within about twenty-five steps of me, and stood in plain view. I did not move, but the javelinas remembered that I had moved. Two retreated; the big boar stood his ground, and champed his tushes five or six times. Then he went out of sight. I stood for a few minutes hoping for another appearance. When I started to move, the three javelinas rushed with snorts out of a bush very near me. The sow and her pig had not come into sight after fleeing the first time. It was the presence of the pig, no doubt, that made the boar and his associates somewhat aggressive. There are true tales of javelinas' treeing hunters. This is the only time that one of them ever stood his own ground for me.

The two best things about deer-hunting, for me at any rate, are the side experiences and the sense of expecting. To sit in a tree and hear the wind—and expect; to lie down by a tank and notice how all animals, both wild and domestic, look when a hard-shelled turtle falls off a bank into water with a splash—and to expect; to creep down a brush draw, trying to avoid making a single scratching sound, pausing to listen to the scolding of two mockingbirds and a curve-billed thrasher over in a clump of bushes and to wonder if they see a rattlesnake—and to expect; to come upon the drag of an armadillo's tail in the sand—this is to live with all the senses. This is what getting out means. Just about any time of the year is in season and it won't matter most of the time if the firing-pin has dropped out of the gun.

I have just come from a camp down in the Brush Country, in Maverick County, to be specific. Some of the time I was alone; some of the time Edgar Kincaid, Jr., was with me. In that part of the thorned world there are open hills, stretches of the original prairie. Sandhill cranes want prairie country to light on and feed in; I have never seen or heard of one in brush. This December I saw and heard more sandhill cranes than I have noted anywhere since a visit I made to Babícora Ranch in southern Chihuahua years ago.

The country I was camped in is watered mainly by enormous tanks. At dusk one evening we saw fifty or more sandhill cranes settle down at the edge of a tank. Years ago an old Mexican told me that they often spent the night on a little island in a river running through his ranch, so as to be safe from coyotes and other enemies. Without any available island, they seem to like the water's edge. There they have only one side to guard, the water protecting the other. If water is shallow, they may stand out in it. One night about 10 o'clock while I was trying to glimpse pack rats that seemed to have the idea of carrying off an empty water bucket, I heard the cranes fluting their lonesome cries up in the sky somewhere. I wondered if they had been disturbed on their ground roost, and I wondered if in the dark they could find another place to settle. If not, they might keep on flying till daylight, I suppose, for they have great endurance, coming from Canada or Alaska in winter.

They get up early, and at times you can hear them before day-light. That's the richest time in camp for sounds. One dawn while drinking coffee, I heard their music. Before that coyotes had carried the tune. Then there was silence and two big owls went to talking to each other from trees below the tank at which we camped. They were not hooting; they were talking in dove-like tones, adding to the serenity and freshness of morning. With the coming of light, a variety of small birds went to chirping. I did not want to leave camp at all; the goodness of nature seemed to be seeping into me.

At noon my old friend Luke Stillwell and his wife came to have dinner with us, bringing cake and fried chicken. He is a government trapper but understands a lot more about animals than the business of destroying them. While we were watching a long snake-like line of cranes flying south and listening to their fluting, he said they were now getting fat and deliciously flavored on wild onions. I had noticed little excavations on the prairies and wondered who made them. That afternoon I and Edgar Kincaid, Jr., whose knowl-edge of and delight in birds are extraordinary, examined the ground from which a flock of cranes had just flown and found that they had pulled up many wild onions and husked them before swallow-ing them. The wild onions taste more like garlic than onions. The grass-like leaves from the bulbs, which grow in clusters like shallots, are just now pushing above ground. I had a notion of killing one of the cranes and cooking it so as to experience the wild onion flavor in its flesh, but decided that any creature giving me and others so much pleasure by being alive should never die by my hand. Its leisurely, majestical stalking about is as delightful as its flying. It seems never to feed greedily or hurriedly. Some members of any flock on the ground always have their heads up and are looking.

Luke Stillwell told about finding a "large white-breasted hawk" on the ground with a dark coachwhip snake wrapped twice around its neck and under its wings. The hawk had killed the snake by bit-ing its head, but the body of the snake still had .life in it. Luke Stillwell thinks the hawk would have freed itself in time, but he unwrapped the snake. The hawk flew away only a short distance and rested. Edgar Kincaid, Jr., thinks the hawk was probably the ferruginous rough-leg, called also prairie eagle and eagle hawk. He is a noble fellow and is properly protected by law. He no doubt gets scores of rats and other rodents to one snake. I would not want to hunt deer where there were no wood rats, no hawks, no varmints to make tracks, no coyotes to serenade the world.

In camp we "sat down with the greatest philosopher in the world, the fire." I like the campfire when it is blazing and lighting up the bushes around. I like it when the coals are dying under thin white ashes. I like it in the morning before breakfast. I like the smells of wood and coffee and boiled beans and roasting venison ribs that go with it. I like its brightness and I like its shadows. I like talk by it and I like silence beside it. It is the core of camp and the kernel of a hunting trip.

At dusk I was driving my car, on the seat with me a friend from Boston and the manager of the Maverick County ranch where I often hunted. We had just crossed a gullied draw when I saw a buck deer topping over the hill in front of us and coming right down the road. It was a winding dirt road, but at this particular stretch was straight. We had seen seventeen other deer that afternoon, mostly on grounds where cottonseed cake was being fed to steers, near waterings. These deer would have been visible to anyone who passed along. They were after particles of cottonseed cake left in the grass by the cattle. About twenty minutes before this we had sighted a ranch feed truck taking the road ahead of us and we were saying that it had probably scared all the deer away. We were not hunting; we were just enjoying seeing wild, free things.

The instant I sighted the buck, I stopped the car and killed the engine. At first I considered letting the engine idle, for after a deer has seen a car move and heard the engine, its purr often excites more curiosity than fear. This buck had neither seen nor heard us. There was no wind. He kept coming right down the road, sometimes trotting. He was perhaps four hundred yards away when he came into view. Evidently he was not seeing us at all, though our car was in full view.

In dim light anyone looking uphill skylights an object and has a strong advantage over anyone looking downhill without any light behind the object. The darkest darkness I have ever experienced was while riding a horse down a mountain trail one night in starlight. Everything under and ahead of me and the horse was pitch black. There was no horizon except up the mountain, behind us.

This buck could not, I believe, see our stationary car below him. We were stopped between mesquites on both sides of us. Furthermore, the buck's senses had probably been dulled by much running around after does.

When he was about halfway down the hill, an airplane passed rather high up and almost over us. The buck sidled slightly into thin brush lining the road, but did not halt. When he came to where the leafless mesquites were a little thicker, he preferred travelling next to them rather than in the middle of the road. He was no longer trotting. We could see the long prongs of his antlers; he had only eight points, but the horns were exceptionally long, and when fat he would have made an excellent buck.

He came to within not more than 25 steps of the car, paused slightly as if recognizing an inconvenient barrier, and then walked into the brush to the left of us. He soon passed through a little opening on that side not 30 steps away. He came closer to me than any other buck not hot after a doe has ever come. I have no doubt that he had seen the truck ahead of us and after it passed had started down the road to the feeding ground.

We were lucky in being near this feeding ground at dusk, in there being no wind to carry our scent, and in being downhill, but if we had not seen him first, had not stopped noiseless and remained noiseless and motionless, taking every advantage of our chance, we should never have seen him at such close range.

Another year I hunted on this same ranch with my cousin Dudley Dobie of San Marcos, who is a good camp man and a great lover of everything outdoors. Our first "adventure," as he called it, was with a coon. We were camped beside a dirt tank in a wooden shack in which a truck load of cottonseed cake had been stored. The first night was too cold for anything to stir, though the cold did not make the deer run. The season was still too early. The second night a coon awakened us intermittently by gnawing on cottonseed cake he had torn out of a sack. When a light was thrown on him, he would scamper out a broken window and under an old screen that he or somebody else had torn loose. Then we could hear him objecting under the house. There were two openings into this cottonseed cake room from the one in which we slept.

The next day, we boarded up the lower part of the broken screen, but that night heard Mr. Coon scratching at it. A lighted kerosene lantern on a can by the window deterred him, but increased his under-the-floor activities. He seemed to be trying to knock out a floor block. I could not tell whether he was using his head, his tail or an arm for a hammer. With a flashlight we got several glimpses of him beneath the house. I thought that coons laid up by day and rustled a living outside at night. This one was cake-hungry, did not bother meat, and spent the forepart of each night making noises under the floor. He became a cherished familiar.

He was not so familiar, however, as a cactus wren that rustled around the outdoor kitchen by day and was much bolder than the white-crowned sparrows for whom we put out bread crumbs several times a day. One noon when we came in, we found a blue (scaled) quail in the house, utterly exhausted from having beaten himself against a window trying to get out. He had entered through an open door. Coveys of both blue quail and bobwhites passed the camp daily on their way to water at the tank. The spirit of the tank was a great blue heron, who talked at night. Associated with him in catching fish and frogs was a fine kingfisher, who could hover stationary for a whole minute in one place over a spot of water he was watching. All the rest of my life I shall be seeing him hovering there in the air, as often in recollection I see a kestrel of Kew Gardens hovering while I lie on the grass and watch him and watch pilotless bombs tear across the sky to destroy London.

One hot afternoon I, with the unsportsman-like idea of waylaying a buck, hid myself behind a sprangly mesquite bush growing on the dam of a big tank. The first person who came along was a lone steer in surly mood. He had drunk, but for half an hour he stood where the deer were supposed to come down to drink and bur-bur-burred to himself. It would be imprecise to say that he was thinking, but some instinct within seemed to be expressing outrage at his lost bullhood. Finally he left, and a striped-back skunk, as independent as any bull, came to the margin of the water, drank all he wanted, and went away. Meanwhile two sandhill cranes that I could see out on an open space of ground, beyond a rim of brush enclosing my side of the tank, kept raising their lone cries. They kept stalking about very slowly. In this region I have seen hundreds of cranes alight to eat wild onions. This dry year no wild onions had sprouted and twenty-nine cranes in low, long-fluting flight were the most I saw.

By the time the steer had talked himself out, the skunk had his fill, and the cranes had left, the sun was low. It was directly in my eyes, its reflection in the water making a double glare. Then I saw three deer—a doe and two yearlings—bounding through the brush. They met a doe and a yearling I had not seen and all five came to the water, hardly fifty feet from me, and drank. The does drank longer and looked up more frequently than the yearlings, but at one time all five were drinking, no sentinel watching. They placed their delicate front feet only in the margin of the water; they did not wade into the mud as cattle wade. For minutes, after drinking, they remained on the short-cropped, half-green bermuda grass near the water, cropping a little and moving about at leisure. Then a doe and yearling trotted around the end of the dam and drank hastily. All seven deer were still in sight when I saw two more away across the tank, maybe three hundred yards off. They were out some distance from the water and had probably drunk before I glimpsed them. I watched them through glasses.

When I turned back from them to the spot I was waylaying, a small four-pronged buck was finishing his drink. The only reason for shooting him was to eat. I am very fond of venison. Now he was looking intently at my hiding place. If I made the least move, he would see me and in a few bounds be out of sight. He turned tail to me and started walking directly into the sun. I got my rifle ready and was simply blinded by the sun, which for weeks and months had not had a cloud over it. I shot anyway and missed.

Now the cattle had all left the tank and, of course, all the deer. The sun would soon be down. I still hoped to see a real buck come in. Twilight had dimmed into darkness when I saw a good-sized deer come from around the end of the dam. It was suspicious. The wind had shifted. I could not make out in the faded light whether this deer wore horns or not. I thought not. When it came to the water I saw by the reflection that it was a doe and that she was looking directly at me. After I saw the reflection I could not see the animal itself. I was looking downward to the darkened earth, had no way of skylighting. The only way I knew the doe was drinking was by the shadow. There she was, standing upside down, drinking from under the water instead of from over it.

As soon as she withdrew she gave a snort and, I judged, left the country. She had caught my smell. It was time for me to withdraw. The coyotes were singing. They were still sporadically crying when I got to camp. "I hope they will always be in this country," Dudley Dobie said. I hope so too. Dudley had a fat buck to show.

My ideal has always been the hunter whose "step than the red deer's was freer and lighter," whose "eye than the eagle's was keener and brighter." Neither my step nor my eye has ever been such. There is no use pretending. I am enormously fond of venison, but I guess I am fonder of expecting. I shan't forget the doe drinking in the darkness upside down.

CORRER DEL PAISANO

THERE used to be lots of tramps passing through the Thicket. They were usually woolly-looking creatures with a broomstick over their shoulders and all their belongings tied up in a bundle attached to the end of it. Aunt Min fed most of the tramps who stopped and asked for a handout because she was afraid if she didn't, she "might be aturning away angels unawares." Most of these folks would offer to draw some water, chop some wood or do any chore that one might have for them. One day when Aunt Min was sitting on the front gallery piecing quilt blocks, she looked up and saw this "paddy" coming across the yard. When he reached the gallery he said, "Good morning, Ma'am, . . . if you would be so kind as to give me a handout, I'll tell you something that will do you and your daughters and your daughter's daughters good all the days of your lives." This was a different approach and Aunt Min decided to fix him a plate without requiring a chore. When the tramp had finished eating he said, "Always knot your thread Ma'am, and you'll never lose stitches."

Lois Williams Parker
Beaumont, Texas

WHY I CURSED GOD

Mody C. Boatright

SOON after my sixth birthday—
and that was while the century was young—the pastor of the Cumberland Church of Sweetwater, Texas, announced that on a Sunday soon to come, his pulpit would be occupied by a guest minister, who would preach a sermon especially for the children. When that Sunday came my mother saw that I was seated in one of the front pews which the children were invited to occupy, in dark suit and white blouse, hair brushed and shoes shined.

I do not remember the minister's name. I recall him now as a man with dark whiskers who could have been mistaken for General Grant. If he announced a text, I took no note of it. I remember nothing he said until he exhibited his stage properties. One of these was an immense spider—or as I now suspect, a model of one—bigger than any tarantula I had seen around rocky places in the pastures. He held it up dangling from a string and must have talked about it, but I cannot recall what he said. I have often wondered since whether it had any connection with either Bruce or Dean Swift.

It was another set of props that made the sermon memorable. These consisted of a glass of clear liquid I assumed to be water, and two bottles, one containing a clear liquid and the other a black one like ink. He set the glass on the pulpit and told us that it was like our souls inside us were when we were born—his branch of the church had long ago repudiated the doctrine of infant damnation—

pure and clean and bright. He said, though, that even when very young, we were inclined to sin, to do things which we should not do, and he would show us what this would do to our souls. He removed the stopper from the bottle of black liquid and poured some into the glass. A dark cloud formed which soon spread through the mass, making it look like ink. This, he said, is what sin does to people—made them all dark and ugly inside. He paused a while looking sadly at the ugliness he had created. Then he turned to us smiling and assured us that we did not have to stay that way. If we were sorry that we sinned and asked Him to, God would forgive us and make us clean again; he would show us what would happen. Here he uncorked the bottle of clear liquid and poured some into the glass. A clear cloud formed and soon spread through the mass making it as transparent as it was before he poured in the black liquid.

The turning of clear liquid into dark was commonplace enough. I had seen it happen sometimes when I washed my hands. But the turning of dirty water into clean was something else. I had never seen it before. It must be a miracle like turning water into wine. I could readily imagine what happened inside me as I sinned, was sorry, and was forgiven. What I looked like inside was no mystery. I had seen beeves butchered on the ranch. After the offal was removed there was the rib case a delicate pink with faint light stripes where the ribs showed through. As I sinned black spots would appear and spread over the surface, then as I was sorry and asked for forgiveness, the darkness would go away and my insides would be pink again. The process was a fascinating one, and I was eager to feel it in operation.

Perhaps the minister mentioned some childish sins such as disobedience to parents, idleness in school, fighting with playmates and the like, but these sins were hardly impressive enough, and I wondered what was the worst sin a boy could commit. I don't know whether I knew the story of Job or not, but for some reason I decided that the worst thing a boy could do was to curse God.

Sometimes when my father bumped his head on the mantel he would say "dog on the mantel." or if he was roping calves and missed a throw, he would say "dog on." And this I thought was cursing. So for the next few days as I went about my business I would think and sometimes whisper, "Dog on the Lord." Then my inside would turn black. Then I would say "I'm sorry, God; forgive me," and my inside would be clean again. I would say these things faster and faster, so that black and pink succeeded each other like the flashing on and off of a light.

The fun ended sometime later as a result of a remark I made to my sister several years my senior. I did not tell of my experiment, but in another context I remarked that one need not make any great effort to be good, for no matter what you did, if you were sorry and asked Him to, God would forgive you. Without denying God's power of forgiveness, she gave me a lecture on the wickedness of sinning in the expectation of being forgiven. It must have been effective, because I never cursed God again.

CORRER DEL PAISANO

AN Irishman (Pat, I suppose) attended mass and was very much impressed with the sermon, which was on the subject of the last judgment. Deeply thoughtful he caught up with the priest as he walked away from the church, and said, "Father, if it wouldn't be troublin' ye too much, I'd like to be askin' ye a few questions."

"Surely, Pat, my son. Go ahead."

"Father, ye were afther sayin' that folks is gonna be there from all times and all kinds o' places, is that right?"

"We are given to understand, yes."

"And, Father, do ye be tellin' me that both Cain and Abel will be there an' both o' thim at the same time?"

"I believe the scripture states it that way."

"And David and that big slob Goliath?"

"I so read it."

"And Brian Boru and Cromwell?"

"That is true, we are taught."

"Thin, Father, all I've got to say is there'll be domn little judgin' done that first day."

Martha Emmons
Waco, Texas

"Ranch Life" by Frank Reeves

PHOTOGRAPHY & TEXAS TRADITIONS

Ronnie C. Tyler

WHEN the Amon Carter Museum of Western Art opened its doors to the public in January, 1961, it had a distinguished collection of western paintings and sculpture by Frederic Remington and Charles M. Russell and a building designed by architect Philip Johnson of New York that was a monument in itself. But the museum was still searching for its identity, for its role as a museum. It was a museum of western art, but no one was certain what that meant. Mrs. J. Lee Johnson III, the chairman of the museum board and daughter of Mr. Carter, defined it as "not eastern" for a reporter from *Time Magazine,* leaving the staff of the museum a broad area in which to work.

The identity problem arose because "the West" is a peculiarly American phenomenon in which reality and fiction frequently blend. Nor was it ever a definite geographical area, but moved from east to west with the frontier. The West might be any point from the Atlantic coast to the Pacific, depending upon the time period.

Working within what certainly appears to be a loose definition, the museum board of trustees then set out to develop a "new kind of museum" that could take advantage of the many opportunities for research and education in the numerous subjects that find their identification as "western." To painting and sculpture Director Mitchell A. Wilder soon added photography. "As a museum with a basic interest in the arts," he wrote soon after he arrived in Fort

21

Worth, "every effort is made to interpret the exhibition through creative media—painting, sculpture, and photography . . . . In the opinion of the museum, the arts of the West are many and are all fair game for its purpose." The expansion of the museum program to include photography, said Wilder, was "so natural as to need no comment."

Once photography was a part of the program, it was only a matter of time until the museum turned to Texas for some of its exhibitions. During the ten year existence of the museum there have been five photographic exhibitions related almost exclusively to Texas: Todd Webb's "Texas Houses of the Nineteenth Century," Frank Reeves's "Ranch Life," Shel Hershorn's "A Personal Country," Diane Hopkins' "Photographic Metaphor," and Michael Kostiuk's "The Big Thicket: A Way of Life."

All the photographic exhibitions fit the pattern that Beaumont Newhall, former director of George Eastman House and now visiting professor of photographic history at the University of New Mexico, outlined for contemporary photography. Contemporary photography, he explained, is a combination of various styles developed over the last half century: straight photography, formalistic photography, documentary photography, and a term that Alfred Stieglitz called the "equivalent." Straight photography Newhall defined as being an exact image. Whatever thought the picture conjures up in the mind of the viewer, there is never any doubt as to what the subject of the photograph is. The formalistic style is concerned with the search for organization and form for their own sake. Usually the picture is one in which these elements have been discovered accidentally, such as in nature. Documentary photography is usually intended for publication. Journalists most often are documentary photographers. The effort is placed on communication, telling about something, recording without intrusion, and informing honestly. The photographer many times is also trying to convince the viewer of a point of view. The final form that Newhall discussed is what he called the equivalent, a term borrowed from Stieglitz. In this instance the photographer has other meanings he is trying to convey through the subject of the picture. The photograph is used as a metaphor. All of these elements have been involved in the five exhibitions that the Carter Museum has presented.

"Texas Houses of the Nineteenth Century" by Todd Webb

"Door: Mission Estrada" by Diane Hopkins

"Reflections on Floor" by Diane Hopkins

"Sand Dunes" by Diane Hopkins

The first exhibition the museum sponsored on a Texas subject was "Texas Homes of the Nineteenth Century," a product of the Texas Architectural Survey, jointly sponsored by the museum and the School of Architecture of the University of Texas at Austin. The stimulus for the project, which began in 1964, was the realization that some of the most significant objects of the past are architectural, and that they are being obliterated at a rapid rate. John C. Garner, Jr., carried out field research in 1964 and 1965. Todd Webb, well-known photographer from Santa Fe, New Mexico, photographed the buildings designated by Garner. In 1966 the museum exhibited the photographs and the University of Texas Press published them in a book of the same title, authored by Drury Blakeley Alexander.

The emphasis of the Texas Architectural Survey was simply to record the best examples of nineteenth century Texas architecture, or straight photography. As former University of Texas Chancellor Harry H. Ransom, then a member of the Carter Museum board, explained, the desire was to document a part of the heritage of the state. We are now aware of "a past which we have come at last to cherish," he noted.

Documentary photography—or journalistic photography—is probably the most popular form of the art today, and most of the museum's Texas shows fall into that category. The first such exhibit, the work of Frank Reeves, was presented in 1965. Longtime livestock editor of the Fort Worth *Star Telegram*, Reeves began taking pictures to accompany his reporting in 1912. He documented three segments of the cattle industry of Texas and the Southwest: ranch life at work, ranch life at play (rodeos), and personalities. By eating, sleeping, and living with the cowboys, Reeves was able to obtain the candidness and honesty that he demanded in his pictures. By knowing the nature of animals, he was able to anticipate their moves and get some of the finest action shots without being hit or injured. Reeves started his photographic career with a mail-order camera when he was sixteen. He continues it today, taking many pictures to accompany his popular "Chuck Wagon" column in the *Star-Telegram*.

Shel Hershorn, a Dallas free-lance photographer, traveled through West Texas gathering images for "A Personal Country," a documen-

"The Big Thicket" by Michael Kostiuk

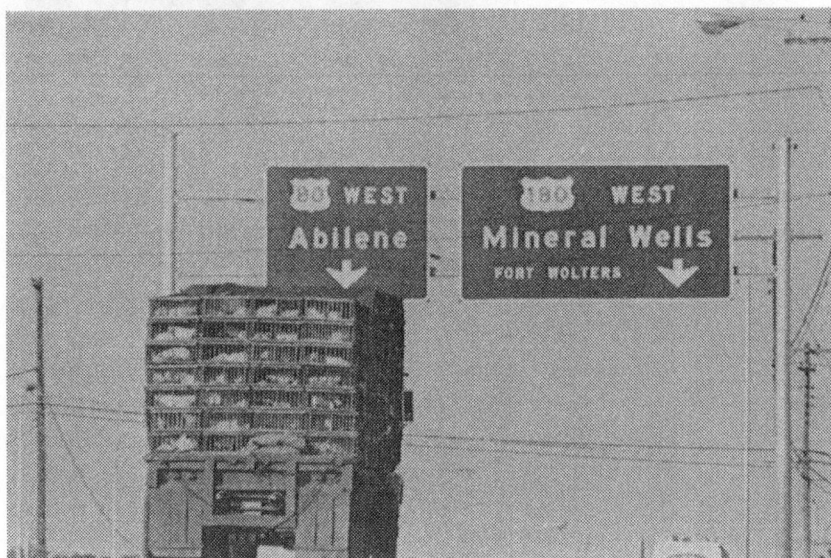

"A Personal Country" by Shel Hershorn

tary record of present-day West Texas based on A. C. Greene's semi-autobiographical book of the same title. The pictorial essay portrays various aspects of West Texas life. "It's a kind of an insider's view, and an outsider's view," explained Greene. "It presents West Texas the way it is and, in a sense, the way it was." Greene, the insider, interpreted the country for Hershorn, the outsider, and directed him to particularly significant sites for photography. But Hershorn himself reacted to what he saw, thus presenting the outsider's viewpoint. Hershorn saw the dominant factors of life: religion, economy, communication. He saw the reaction of the people to the harsh climate—the wind, the cold northers, the droughts. But he caught their determination, their particular spirit.

One of the museum's Texas exhibitions probably could be classified under Stieglitz's category of the equivalent, or metaphor. Diane Hopkins, an assistant professor of design and art at Southern Methodist University, treated familiar objects in an original and creative manner through the highlighting of texture, form, lighting, etc. Centering on subjects on the Gulf Coast, the Big Bend, and in the Dallas and Wichita Falls areas, Miss Hopkins said that she had been working with what she considered to be the "more subtle beauty of Texas" for several years. "I want other people to see what I see," she explained. "I'm convinced that if you look hard enough, there are interesting things all around you." This she proved with her exhibition of Dallas freeways, lonely and deserted cabins in the Big Bend, wind-whipped trees on a West Texas golf course, sand dunes along the coast.

Another Dallas photographer, Michael Kostiuk, Jr., focused on Texans who live near one of the nation's last wilderness areas, the Big Thicket. In an exhibition entitled "The Big Thicket: A Way of Life," Kostiuk took a visitor's look at the Thicket and its people. "I simply walked in and started shooting" he said. "This may not work for a writer, but I've found that it does for a certain kind of photographer, and I hope the proof is in the pictures I shot with the sense that the facade of a people, their faces and clothes and buildings, can be an expression of their inner selves." Kostiuk's study of a few months reflects a history that dates back a century and a half, and one that depends as much on legend as on written record. Centered in portions of Jefferson, Liberty, Polk, and Hardin counties, the Big Thicket long was a historical no-man's-land. But it is also, according to scientists, a biological crossroads. It soon became known as a hunter's paradise, with many deer, bear, and some panthers.

Beginning in the town of Kountze, Kostiuk toured the highways and sandy back roads of the region. He visited in towns, homes, and businesses. He prowled through the back roads and the underbrush. The exhibition was his personal look at the people of the Thicket. Like Walker Evans, Kostiuk shows in his pictures that something that is peculiarly American, particularly rural American.

The Amon Carter Museum of Western Art is continually searching for new artists and new styles in photographing western scenes and traditions. Future photographic exhibitions planned for the museum are "Texas Civil Architecture of the Nineteenth Century" and "The Big Bend."

A camera in the hands of a good photographer can do many things in the recording of the folklore and traditions of a people and place. It can document and freeze an actual moment of actual people engaged in their work or play. This is important. The scientific and technical details of how things are done must necessarily be recorded to satisfy the curiosity of later generations, or perhaps to show them the way. Photography can also interpret the lives of the folk. A camera in the hands of a true artist responds like a paint brush, displaying the subtle shades of light and dark that life is made from. A sensitive photographic artist, like a great painter, captures the universal, the timelessness in a point of time. He stimulates the emotions and imagination of the viewer as much as a Rembrandt or Remington.

GOD'S COUNTRY

When the foundations for the world were laid
they quit at noon in Texas,
meaning to return to finish up the job,
but something intervened;
they went away and left it as it was,
and that is how it is.

I rate them as good workmen on the whole,
judging from what I've seen:
Virginia they designed for landscape painters;
laid out New England to be quaint and picturesque,
with spots for antique shoppes later on;
scraped South Dakota level for the plow;
Iowa, I guess, was meant for hogs and corn;
when they made Oklahoma they were tired.

Texas is different;
here the materials of creation
lie piled and scattered,
profuse, but rough and still unfinished
(perhaps they found the job too big
and meant to come back later with more tools).

In Texas
the high plains roll against the Rockies,
breaking in places south and west,
beyond the Pecos,
in the Big Bend,
where rivers flow in gorges
and each little stream
cuts an arroyo all its own.

Texas is wind-blown prairies, purple hills,
bright sun, blue shadows, and clear air;
land where the longhorns roam and mustangs run,
where coyotes sing the silver stars
and golden eagles soar
from rough red rocks into a smooth blue sky.

God's country must be nice; too nice I fear.
You can have God's country; I like it here.

Martin Staples Shockley
Denton, Texas

RETURN TO PIN HOOK

William A. Owens

On a Sunday morning, before people were stirring, I walked past the store and schoolhouse at Pin Hook, Texas, and stopped at the graveyard long enough to read inscriptions on the few gravestones. Among them was

> Remember, friend, as you pass by
> As you are now so once was I;
> As I am now so you shall be;
> Prepare, dear friend, for eternity.

Then I went to where our house had stood, now a place of emptiness. The barn was still there, but it was beginning to lean as logs rotted away. It was a homestead abandoned, the yard and garden now grazed by cattle. Thirty years or so before, my father had built there in the shade of oaks. The oaks spread their branches farther and farther out. The well he had dug with pick and shovel still yielded good water, but had started caving in. A few more years and all the signs of his work would be gone.

I crossed the road and walked the fields that Wiley Witherspoon had cleared and worked while Texas was still a part of Mexico. Toward Little Pine Creek he had built his house and barns and quarters for the slaves he had brought with him. All but one building had rotted back into the earth. It was a square cabin, built of

31

logs on which I could still see the marks of ax and broadax, the spaces between the logs chinked with post-oak clay held together with grass from the fields. It now had a rough board floor, added later perhaps when the cabin was moved farther up the creek. In this house my father's mother was born.

It was easy in these silent fields to wonder what compulsion, what hope of reward made Wiley Witherspoon and his wife load their four daughters and belongings on a wagon and, with others in a train, make the long journey, beginning in Kentucky or Tennessee, across Arkansas, and a hundred miles into Texas, to this spot. What had made them choose this spot when there were so many acres open for choosing? The land had belonged to the Indians and they had used it. In gullies close to the creek I could still find arrowheads and pieces of clay pots. For the Indians it was good land. Away from the creek it was wooded, with an upper canopy of oaks mixed with hickory and here and there a black walnut, with a lower canopy of huckleberry and other bushes. Along the creek there were dense cane brakes, where deer and buffalo came to graze.

Wiley Witherspoon came quietly in 1834. He labored and accumulated for fifteen years, and with his wife left as quietly in 1849. He cleared the land. Any other marks he had left had now disappeared, and his name with them except where it appeared on land grants and a will, documents that he had lived there and prospered under the flags of Mexico, Texas, and the United States, and was no doubt left alone by all three.

A little farther on I came to the Witherspoon graveyard on a knoll back from the creek. Here, among some smaller ones, was a small granite marker, bearing the name of Catherine Duval, my great grandmother, the marker put there by her daughter Harriet Wiley Hall. The graveyard yielded its own story. Here were buried the four daughters of Wiley Witherspoon, three of them dead while Pin Hook was still wilderness. Here also lay John M. Hall, who by some circumstance drifted down from New York City, where he was born, met and married Catherine Witherspoon, fathered children, and died, still probably in his thirties. Near him lay his only son, James, who did not live beyond childhood. Near him also lay William Duval, Catherine's second husband, and their daughter

Melinda, my grandmother, who was married at fifteen, a mother at sixteen, and dead at seventeen. The graveyard was far off the road and the graves had settled down to brush-covered earth under black locust trees.

The black locusts had their own story, handed down from generation to generation. The child of one of the Witherspoon slaves died and there was no separate place to bury it. The mother was allowed to bury her child in a corner of the family graveyard. She marked the grave with a small black locust. After the graveyard was abandoned the locust spread and became a grove, in winter, black, gnarled trees against the sky, in spring, a cloud of snowy blossoms sweet on the air, drawing wild bees from tree hollows all up and down Little Pine Creek.

I wondered how master and slave lived and shared in what had to be cramped quarters of the wilderness, what tensions they developed, what tenderness. Another story told me a little. A preacher passing through on horseback agreed to hold a meeting in the master's house. There was no church and preaching was seldom heard. A slave, old Aunt Minerva, was as hungry as anyone else to hear the Gospel, but it was not fitting for her to be in the house with the preacher and the white folks. It was finally decided that she could sit on a chair behind the door where she would not be seen. The preacher began preaching with all the fervor of a frontier evangelist. Aunt Minerva got happier and happier. When she could hold in no longer she burst from behind the door and shouted and danced until she was worn out. Then, like a member of the family, she listened to the preacher till the last amen.

In 1865, June'Teenth the exact date in Texas, the separation between masters and slaves came, and the slaves moved to their own settlement to the north and west of Pin Hook. There, in a school that was part of the Pin Hook district, I might find boys and girls whose ancestors made the journey into the wilderness as slaves of Wiley Witherspoon. I had no desire to go. I had been there before and seen how they lived, in boxing plank cabins, poor, illiterate, slaves in another sense, needing the care of whites who took little heed of them. They had owned no land, left no record.

I found myself looking back over four generations of life in Pin Hook. I was the fifth. No one remembered how it came to be called

Pin Hook, but the name had been known a long time, perhaps for nearly a century—or why, as a joke on a place at the back end of nowhere. In a hundred years life had changed little—for many not at all. The life cycle might still be as short as forty years: birth, marriage, death, the years between filled with a little schooling, much hard work on worn-out land, begetting of children who would begin the cycle all over again.

The day was, I realized, another journey in search of myself, of trying to find out what spark from what generation had sent me away from Pin Hook, what spark had brought me back, what spark made me content to be back. If not a spark, then a chemistry of the soil? I could see the boys and girls in my grades following the life cycles of their parents, too many hookworm kids begetting too many hookworm kids. In me the cycle had been broken, by what I did not know.

Of one thing I was sure: What had happened to me might happen to someone else. My job was to discover and to prompt. Back at the schoolhouse I went through lessons and recesses and talks after supper. The answer to where they were going, when there was an answer was, "I got this old piece o' wore-out land I got to hang onto"; the women, quicker to answer said, "I got people buried here. It wouldn't be right, going off and leaving them." A thing just as sure: Pin Hook was full of porch sitters and store sitters. "If you got a living," they said, "you dast not leave it." They said it with a fear of the unknown, a fear I had seen in the eyes of their children, and in the eyes of people on starvation in Dallas.

THE FOLKLORE OF TEXAS FEUDS

C. L. Sonnichsen

BACK in the early thirties, for reasons which have never been quite clear to me, I became a specialist in the feuds of Texas, and ever since then I have collected vendettas as other people collect ancient guns or vintage automobiles. I am probably the only one of my kind, for feuds are dangerous and difficult things to handle, but I have no regrets. I have learned a great deal about human history and human nature and have made contact with some of the finest people one could ever hope to meet—the sons and daughters of the feuding clans of Texas.

First of all, I learned that to study feuds is to study folklore. They, more than any other human activity, are an expression of the "traditional customs and beliefs . . . preserved unreflectively among a people" which by definition constitute folklore. They are folklore in action.

Furthermore, they follow patterns that are as old as mankind— patterns which we have spent thousands of years trying to get rid of with only indifferent success and which we repeat, step by step, whenever conditions are right. They teach us that in all of us the old primitive instincts are present, just below the surface, ready to take over when we are frightened, or abused, or driven beyond the limit of endurance.

Before attempting to tell what a feud is or isn't, and how it operates, it might be well to look at a sample. There were at least a hundred feuds in Texas, some of them lingering on for as much as thirty years; some involving hundreds of people and dozens of deaths. A typical example would be the terrible outlaw feud north and east of Austin in the seventies and early eighties. The village of McDade was a focal point, and one of several climaxes came in the form of a multiple hanging in 1883.

McDade is now a wide place in the road thirty-eight miles east of Austin at the edge of an area of post oaks and bottomland which is still pretty rough and rugged. A sort of infection center in the early days was the district known as "The Knobs" from three good-sized green hills ten or twelve miles north of McDade. In the shadow of The Knobs was the Blue or Blue Branch community where terrible deeds were done in the early days and where a man could probably still get a fight if he wanted one badly enough.

As early as 1868 stories appeared in print hinting at bands of horse thieves and desperadoes hanging out in this region. When McDade became a railhead in the fall of 1871, boomtown life on a small scale was added to the ordinary perils of existence. The thugs in the thickets increased and multiplied, robbed cotton farmers on their way home with their crop money, and rustled cattle and horses by the hundreds. In those days the big cattlemen kept bands of tough cowboys who didn't much care what brands were on the hides of the steers they drove off to Kansas. The little cattlemen got even by picking up what the big fellows didn't take care of. Such small-time larceny was something frontier settlers had to expect. What could not be shrugged off was the wholesale stealing of "The Gang."

This Gang—whose members were sometimes called Notch Cutters because they lived out in the post oaks, mostly—was a mysterious organization which went about its business with great caution and cleverness. Its members were loyal and secretive to the death and thought nothing of committing perjury or murder to protect their brothers in crime.

Following the familiar pattern, a counter-organization began to take shape in the middle seventies. In 1874 several supposed criminals were found hanging to trees, and the Gang retaliated whenever it could, bushwhacking horsemen and sending farmers home dead in the bottoms of their ox wagons.

The biggest cattlemen in the region were soon drawn in. Twenty miles or so from McDade lived the Olive family—James Olive and his sons Jay, John, Ira, and Prentice. The latter, called "Print" Olive, was known all over the cattle country in later years. In 1876 he was a tough Texas cattleman who was obviously serious when he said that he and his men "would kill anyone they found skinning their cattle or riding their horses."

On March 22, 1876, the first result of this policy appeared when two men named Turner and Crow were left dead on the prairie beside the Olive beeves they had been skinning. Their bodies were wrapped in the green hides as a warning to anybody who might be interested.

A good deal of skirmishing and night riding followed, culminating on August 1, 1876, in a night attack on a concentration of Olive men camped in the yard of one of their ranch houses. Jay Olive died of wounds received in this fight and several others were hurt. The Olives retaliated and as a result were brought to trial at Georgetown. The situation was very tense as the Olive supporters camped on one side of town and the opposition on the other, scaring unsuspecting travelers and getting ready for civil war. The Olives were acquitted, however, without a fight and Print moved his family and his herds to Nebraska and Kansas, where he made more history.*

Still the robbing and murdering went on. Men were found hanging in the woods, their own stake ropes around their necks. Texas newspapers complained that crime was rampant and that "There have been more men killed in Texas in the last year than she lost during the late war." The McDade region was regarded as about the hottest spot anywhere.

Again desperadoism was met by a counter-organization—perhaps a revival of the vigilante group of 1874. Newspaper reports said that an initiation fee was charged and that the money was used to run down thieves who stole from the members. Of course both

---

*The story of the Olives has been told by Mari Sandoz in *The Cattlemen* (New York: Hastings House, 1958) and by Harry E. Chrisman in *The Ladder of Rivers* (Denver: Sage Books, 1962). Miss Sandoz follows Nebraska tradition in giving the Olives the worst of it. Mr. Chrisman is in general favorable to them.

sides kept their business carefully under cover, but that such an organization existed is proved by what happened next—the mass hanging of 1877 at The Knobs.

At this time Pat Earhart, a man a little out of place in this frontier world, was living out at Blue. He had better clothes and manners than his neighbors, some education, and considerable musical talent. He ran a singing school and played the fiddle for the dances frequently held at his house. Whenever that fiddle began to squeak, all the young bucks in the neighborhood were sure to be there, no matter which side they were on.

The most famous of all Earhart's dances was in full swing on June 27, 1877, when several masked members of the vigilante organization appeared at the front and back doors and told Pat to call out the names of five men who were wanted. Wade Alsup, John Kuykendall, Young Floyd and Beck Scott responded. The fifth man managed somehow to make himself scarce and is said to be running yet.

The four men had arms enough to fight a battle, but their guns were stacked in the lean-to. Besides, they did not seem to realize what was happening. Beck Scott, who was dancing with Fanny Alsup when his name was called, borrowed her fan, remarking, "It will be hot as hell before we get to Giddings." He thought he was being arrested and taken to the county seat. Wade Alsup caught on faster. "You won't need no fan where we're going," he said.

It was about two o'clock in the morning when this happened. The masked men took their prisoners out into the darkness and hanged them to a tree five hundred yards from the house—four on a limb.

For a while the shock of this violent deed worked minor miracles. Jim Floyd, a brother of one of the lynchees, left the country, got religion, and became a preacher. Others may have been frightened into a similar change of heart. But mostly the sinners went on sinning and the righteous continued to lose their lives and their money. By 1883 the time was ripe for another explosion. Several people had been killed, including a harmless old storekeeper and a popular deputy sheriff. The citizens had had enough.

On Dec. 7 two hundred of them assembled openly in the little wooden church at the east end of McDade (the only one in town) to talk about a little righteous hanging. Even now nobody will tell who was there, though all the old-timers could mention names. I myself have never tried to identify a single participant. There are some things I just don't want to know. It is said, however, that the assembly went very thoroughly into the list of men who would have to be got rid of before there could be peace and order in the country, and at least one of those present heard the name of a near relative called out and confirmed while he sat tight, unable to do a thing about it.

The Galveston *News* carried a story about the meeting the next day. It mentioned no names but said the object was to "assist the officers of the law" and described the participants as "the very best citizens."

On Christmas Eve, 1883, the meeting bore fruit. A noisy bunch had assembled in the Nash Brothers' Rock Saloon at McDade. Among them were several members of the Notch Cutters—the old Gang. About 7:30 a group of masked men quietly entered the front door. There were more outside, somewhere between forty and eighty, as the story has been handed down. They never said a word, but each one had a Winchester in the crook of his arm and they nudged three men out of the saloon with those gun barrels—two McLemores and Henry Pfeiffer. The McLemores are said to have been under indictment for cattle theft. Pfeiffer was taken, they say, because he recognized one of the vigilantes in spite of his mask and called his name aloud.

Another man almost went along—a young fellow from Georgia who had come out to see if the West was as wicked as he had been led to believe. Supposing the men were going to a Christmas Eve dance at The Knobs, he trailed along outdoors but was shoved back by the men with rifles. When he found out next day what sort of party he had almost joined, he was so sick he had to go to bed.

The three victims were taken a mile north of town and hanged to a blackjack tree.

The last killings in the feud took place at McDade the next day—Christmas, 1883. Three Beatty boys—Jack, Heywood, and Az—with their kinfolks Byrd Hasley, Robert Stevens, and Charley Goodman, rode in during the morning to do some shopping. They had not heard of the events of the night before, but soon found

out. Some of them became very much excited when they were
told that Heywood Beatty's name had been called by the vigilantes
in the Rock Saloon. They proceeded to call two men to account,
local merchants named George Milton and Tom Bishop. The result was a terrific gunfight in the main street of McDade which
resulted in the death of Az and Jack Beatty and the accidental
killing of an innocent bystander named Willie Griffin. Nineteen-
year-old Heywood Beatty put up a heroic fight and escaped
through the pastures, marked by bullets in seventeen places.

That was the end of the feud. According to legend another mass
meeting was held in McDade at this time and a list of objection-
able people was drawn up. A local doctor was selected as spokesman, and made the rounds, giving the proscribed men ten days to
wind up their affairs. Heywood Beatty was one who left. He went
to ranching out in the plains country near Weatherford and did not
come back for many years. When he did return to settle up some
business, he would not reenter the town. "Boys," he said, "I'm out
of trouble now and I want to stay out. I won't go in there." And
he didn't.

Using the McDade affair as a fairly representative example of the
Texas variety of feud, I can begin to outline some of the things I
have learned about the folklore of the subject.

In the first place there is a set of ideas which might be called
false folklore which has to be got out of the way at the start. These
are the ideas which pop into everybody's mind automatically
when somebody says the word *feud.* If these notions have a father,
his name is John Fox, Jr., whose *Trail of the Lonesome Pine, A
Cumberland Vendetta,* and other works were once widely read.
From him, or from the folklore on which he drew, we have come
to take it for granted (1) that a feud is strictly a family affair;
(2) that it flourishes exclusively among hillbilly and backwoods
families; and (3) that it starts from something trivial like a stray
cow or a razorback hog.

The McDade feud shows the proportion of truth in these con-
ceptions.

First, it was a faction rather than a family affair. As was always
the case, family and clan loyalties came into the picture, but they
were by no means the most important element in the pattern. This

was the situation more often than not in the history of Texas feuds. Long and bloody wars have been fought between Southerners and Yankee sympathizers; between racial groups with Anglo-Saxon "Americans" on one side and Mexicans or Germans on the other; between political factions such as the "Reds" and "Blues" in the lower Rio Grande valley; between Prohibitionists and Wets. There was even a feud at Waco, the Baptist stronghold, between earnest church people and a group of Doubting Thomases led by the notorious Brann the Iconoclast. After the feud started, the clans always gathered, but something besides family matters usually pulled the first trigger.

The McDade feud shows also that feudists are not always backwoodsmen or mountain boys. It is true that the Notch Cutters were at home in rough country and were not people of high culture, but better citizens were also involved. When two hundred of the "best people" gather in the village church to take the law into their own hands, the trouble is no longer an example of backwoods brutality.

Finally there is the matter of the trivial cause. At McDade fifteen years of intolerable persecution by a secret and secure gang of thieves and murderers was certainly a major grievance. The old notions, however, are hard to dislodge. The Darnells and the Watsons, according to Mark Twain in *Life on the Mississippi,* had long since forgotten the cause of their quarrel. " . . . some says it was about a horse or a cow—anyway it was a little matter." T. D. Clark, leading Kentucky historian, serves it up again. "Trifling matters" such as "livestock, women, politics, and thievery have been the most common sources of strife."

One wonders why Mr. Clark classifies women and politics as "trifling matters."

What, then, is a feud, and how does it work? In Texas the definition has to be simple and inclusive: "Any prolonged quarrel between families or factions involving blood vengeance."

Feuds were not necessarily outbreaks of lawlessness. Feud law— an eye for an eye—was the first criminal code evolved by mankind and many millennia were needed to make murder a crime against the state instead of against an individual or a family. Like almost every other case on record in the Southwest, the McDade feud shows that intolerable conditions precede the outbreak and that it occurs only when the civil government is not able to provide justice. It then becomes necessary to return to an earlier law. What we get is called "folk justice."

H. H. Bancroft in his Popular Tribunals contends that a vigilance committee aims to "assist the law" and that its action springs from a belief in "the right of the governed at all times to instant and arbitrary control of the government." This, he maintains, is not lawlessness.

The word most often used for the folk concept at work here is "self redress"—a belief in righting one's own wrongs, law or no law. Plenty of people today feel that under certain special conditions, any man who is a man will go into action with fists or .45. Southern gentlemen have traditionally held to this belief, and since a high percentage of Texas pioneers were Southerners, their ideas about self redress, combined with frontier notions of folk justice, gave them a double reason for taking the law into their own hands.

The situation was made more inflammable, of course, because everybody in Texas, including little boys and preachers, carried firearms and used them habitually to kill game and sometimes Indians.

Given, then, a pyramid of intolerable situations and a habit of self redress, and feuds are the natural outcome. They are the result of two sets of compulsions—on the one hand the stimuli which prod the feudist into action; on the other, the taboos which he dare not violate.

The first of the compulsions is the duty of revenge. The "traditional customs and beliefs" by which a man lives compel him to exact blood for blood. When it came to feuding, the Texas town or family was truly a folk. John Wesley Hardin was involved in his youth in the notorious Sutton-Taylor feud. The Taylors were his relatives by marriage. "He could not have held up his head in the county if he hadn't taken it up," one of his supporters once assured me. Half a dozen stories could be told of vows of revenge taken over the body of a murdered father or brother—vows which drew blood every time.

In such situations it was hard for anybody to remain neutral. A man who was strong enough and popular enough could do it, but usually a would-be noncombatant had to pack up and leave the country. He was not necessarily condemned for doing so. A witness, an innocent bystander, and sometimes even a close relative of the principals could run and still keep some of his credit. Tom Elder was a fourteen-year-old boy when he stood on the store gallery at McDade during the final battle on Christmas Day, 1883. He knew he would be called as a witness and maybe get himself into more trouble. He went home as fast as he could, packed up, and pulled out for the Panhandle. He did not come back for sixteen years. "And I didn't get any letters, either," he told me when I interviewed him. He had no feeling that he had done wrong in leaving. He was just playing it safe.

The second compulsion which motivates the feudist is the need to fight with fire. After a couple of revenge killings, all scruples are abandoned. The other side has no conception of honor—our side can't risk giving them an advantage. And pretty soon both factions are shooting from the roadside, surrounding houses at daybreak, taking prisoners out of the jail for midnight hangings, and killing each other like wild animals.

"I don't like that shooting from behind a bush. Why didn't you step into the road?" Colonel Grangerford asked his boy Buck, as Huck Finn tells it. "The Shepherdsons don't, Father. They always take advantage," Buck replied. And the old man made no more objections.

It is only a "scorched earth" policy when one side burns the other out in the dead of winter—one way of getting rid of a dangerous enemy. When a vigilance committee gives a man three days to leave the country and shoots him when he overstays his limit, it is his own fault. He actually committed suicide. When a band of executioners rides off, whooping and singing, after cleaning out a nest of the opposition, there is nothing disgraceful in their mirth. If you had eliminated a nest of rattlesnakes which were threatening you and yours, you would feel like celebrating too.

These characteristic behavior patterns help to explain why a feud cannot be settled by agreement. Truces have been arranged more than once in Texas. They last anywhere from fifteen minutes to a few days. Neither side trusts the other, and the agreements are just "scraps of paper."

Naturally, then, a feud has no brakes. It grows worse and worse until one side is eliminated, or a higher authority steps in and imposes peace. The vigilante feuds of Texas show how it works. Ordinarily they begin with the organization of a group of "whitecaps" or (before the Civil War) Regulators to cope with outlawry. Then the Regulators, victims of what Plato calls "the excess of power," become arrogant and unreasonable just because they can get away with it, and a counter-organization (in early times called Moderators) is formed to moderate the Regulators. In the famous feud of the Regulators and Moderators in East Texas in the 1840's Sam Houston had to bring in the militia or the killing never would have stopped.

How much do the women of the group have to do with all this? Plenty! Women seem to be better natural haters than men. More than once in the history of Texas feuds it was a woman who handed her man a shotgun with a significant look. Before the great riot at Richmond in the fall of 1889, the women of the Jaybird faction appeared on the streets with small bags of sand which they handed to men who might be lacking in "grit." After the shooting is over, it is the women who labor most vigorously to keep the old resentments alive. Fifty years after the end of the feud between the Staffords and the Townsends at Columbus, a woman who had been involved was riding in an automobile with a friend of mine. He stopped to pick up another passenger. "If she gets in, I get out," said the first woman. "We don't ride in the same car with those people."

The men, of course, did the actual fighting, and it is always a man who emerges as the epic hero of the feud. The Heroic Age comes again when a feud breaks out, and the leader who can outwit or outfight the opposition becomes a superhuman figure, a Bill Mitchell, a Scott Cooley, a John Wesley Hardin, regarded by lesser mortals with awe. Stories circulate about him, ballads are sung, and his stature increases as he is given credit for exploits which he never performed. As Ash Upson said of Billy the Kid, the deeds of "meaner villains" are attributed to him and he becomes, to a greater or less degree, a folk hero.

The taboos or prohibitions in feud lore were important as the compulsions. A man lost caste, and sometimes his life, if he violated one of the "don'ts." First was the rule against "talking." People learned not to open their mouths at all, and they were right in keeping still. I know of at least one feud that was started by talebearers who went back and forth between the two camps. And countless killings and enmities were caused by an injudicious word dropped at the wrong time. Even after half a century the people on the inside hate to tell what they know. When they do, they usually demand and get a promise that they will not be quoted.

The wisdom of this attitude appears clearly in a story about the McDade feud. Pete Allen, bushwhacked early in the trouble, was found dead in the road with the print of a bootheel in his face. Twenty years afterward some of his friends or kinsfolk started speculating about who did it and made up their minds that they could fix the blame. The next step was to try to get even. One night somebody roped at the man they suspected and nearly got him—the rope bounced off his shoulder. Before the would-be avenger could try again, another man confessed on his deathbed that he was the one who had stomped Pete Allen's face. Too much talk had nearly brought on more trouble.

The great taboo was against what we now call fraternizing. Our side must have no truck with those low criminals on the other one. And that brings Romeo and Juliet into the picture. The forbidden association becomes a temptation, and some dark night there will be an elopement. I know of three cases of intermarriage—a low percentage, but an interesting one. I know also of women who spoiled a good deal of fun for their daughters by worrying lest every new boyfriend might be a connection of the traditional enemy.

When it is all over, another sort of folklore comes into the picture—a legend-making process which looks retrospectively at the feud with wonder and fascination. Stories go round about the toughness of the town where it all happened. Hempstead is still called Six-Shooter Junction, to the distress of its peaceful inhabitants. The story is told of Columbus that the brakeman on the passenger train which passed through the town always announced the station in trumpet tones: "Columbus! Columbus next! Prepare to meet your God!" And the passengers would crouch down between the seats until all danger was past. The same story is told of Richmond and Coahoma.

Another persistent legend says that feeling is still alive in the feuding town and may break out any minute. When I stopped in Houston to make inquiries about the Jaybird-Woodpecker war at Richmond, a few miles away, I was told that the ladies of the town were still cautious about whom they asked to card parties for fear something might be said over the bridge table. I learned later that the Woodpeckers had all left town in 1890 and nobody was left to create a situation.

A third folk story says that everybody who has asked about the feud has been run out of town. When I visited Cuero in search of Sutton-Taylor lore, I was prepared to have this happen to me. It was a relief to find the townspeople uniformly courteous, kindly, and helpful.

Another characteristic legend is the "whodunit." After any great killing somebody goes to trial, but gossip always says he was taking the rap for the real killer. In 1905, for instance, a feud flared up at Hempstead over the prohibition issue. A young man named Roland Brown went to trial for killing Congressman Pinckney in a riot at the courthouse. But those in the know say that a group of men was posted in the jury room in a sort of tower at one corner of the building and actually fired the fatal shots.

Another familiar question is: "Did he really die?" If the man was a powerful and dangerous leader, there was always a suspicion that a log or a sack of sand was in the coffin instead of a body. A small feud flared up at Richmond after the Jaybirds and Woodpeckers were through in which one of the Mitchell family was involved. He moved up to the northern part of the county, where he eventually died of pneumonia. They brought him back to Dr. Gibson's house near Richmond for the funeral, and all of Dr. Gibson's family saw that he was really buried. The other party, unconvinced, used to ask the Gibsons (who were related to both sides) if they were sure a log had not been buried in that coffin. Years later, when it became necessary to move Mitchell's body, it was found that somebody had already opened the coffin—just to make sure.

Only a few humorous stories have been handed down as part of the feuding annals of Texas—they were nothing to laugh about as a rule. There is the legend of the Young Taylor who had part of his cheek and jaw shot away in a brush with the Suttons. "Is there anything I can do for you?" one of his friends asked. "Well, I *would* like a drink of water," said the wounded man, "but I haven't the face to ask for it."

That is pretty much the pattern of Texas feuds. There was only one big one before 1865—the war of the Regulators and Moderators in the 1840's. The disturbances which followed the Civil War, however, provided a good breeding ground, and feuding flourished through the sixties and seventies. In the eighties the Rangers brought self redress and mob rule under control, but there was a curious revival of feuding in the nineties—small but vicious outbreaks which were hard to put down. Since 1900 only occasional disturbances of this type have occurred—but they *have* occurred and may be expected to occur every now and then. And why not? The last thing a people gets rid of is its equipment of folklore. And feuds are folklore in action.

CORRER DEL PAISANO

GRAMPS had a ghost story he told regular about a feller passing a graveyard, and he looked back and seen a ghost behind him. Well, sir, the spirit, as the Preacher says, moved him and he took off down the road like a cat shot in the behind with rock salt. Grampa would always say he was runnin' like a Steeldust colt. After a couple of miles he was blowin' like he was girted too tight, and he had a shoelace dragging so he risked a look over his shoulder and didn't see nothin' so he pulled up and set down on a log. 'Bout the time he bent over to tie his shoelace Mr. Ghost set down by him and says, "Well, we had a pretty good race, didn't we?"

"Yes, Sir," the feller says, "But it weren't a patchin' to the one we're goin' to have when I get this shoelace tied."

Bill Brett
Hull, Texas

FOLK SONGS & FAMILY TRADITIONS

Patrick B. Mullen

MY grandfather, Benjamin Harrison Mullen, was a ballad singer, a fact of which I was unaware until eleven years after his death. I was visiting relatives in Beaumont, Texas, in the summer of 1971, and my aunt, Mrs. Ocie Vick, who is a second grade schoolteacher, happened to mention that "Big Daddy," the name all of the grandchildren called my grandfather, had written down some old ballads which she still had. She found them in a drawer where she kept many of his belongings. The songs were written on old school examination papers which were yellowed and tattered with age. He had carefully written twelve songs down in longhand with a pencil and signed and dated most of them. The year was 1907. Of course, I was very excited to find these because they gave me a link to the family past.

Some of the writing could barely be made out, and some of the papers had holes which obliterated parts of the songs. No music was included; I do not think my grandfather could read music. Each song was divided into stanzas, but the lines seemed to be determined by the width of the paper rather than end rhymes. I copied down all of the material very carefully and returned the original manuscripts to my aunt. Then I interviewed her at length about the songs, my grandfather, family history, and the sort of life my grandfather lived at the time the songs were written down. I did this in an effort to place the songs in a personal and cultural context. I think the songs can be better understood if I give some information on Big Daddy's life and times.

Benjamin Harrison Mullen was born on White Rock Mountain near Fayetteville, Arkansas, on May 1, 1889. His parents had migrated to Arkansas from North Carolina before the Civil War. His father had come as a young man with his father, and the trip took three months. They found a spring on top of a mountain and made their home there. Big Daddy's father was married twice and had three children by the first wife and ten by the second. Benjamin Harrison was the oldest of the second set. He grew up in the same area of Northwest Arkansas where his father's family had first settled. This is an area commonly known as the Ozarks, for the mountains that extend from Arkansas into Missouri.

Harrison Mullen (as he signed many of the songs, although he was known in my lifetime as Ben) went to school in Arkansas, and when he graduated started teaching. In those days you could teach with a high school education, and he first taught at the age of eighteen, in 1907, the same year he wrote down the songs. He would go to normal school during the summers to maintain his qualifications to teach. It was on normal school examination paper that he wrote down the songs. According to my aunt, he usually taught arithmetic to grades four through high school. All of his pupils would be in one room since he taught in small country schools. The normal school was in Ozark, Arkansas, the county seat of Franklin County, and the rural schools in which he taught were within a thirty mile radius of Ozark.

He taught in Arkansas for several years. He married my grandmother, Hattie Nixon, in August, 1908, in Arkansas. Shortly thereafter they moved to Oklahoma where my grandfather still taught school. From there, they moved to Southeast Texas where my grandfather went to work for an oil company, and except for short periods in Wyoming and Louisiana, they remained in Beaumont, Texas, for the rest of their lives.

This is all family history, but interwoven with it are stories about my grandfather and other ancestors, stories which are a form of folklore, what Mody Boatright called "family saga."[1] Some of the stories mention ballad singing and some provide a vivid picture of frontier life in Arkansas, a picture that gives new understanding of the context of the folk songs and ballads. All too often ballad studies ignore the other forms of folklore, superstitions, folktales, legends, and family anecdotes which are a part of the context of folk ballads and songs. As Mody Boatright says, "An event in the family saga has a relation to a social context and reflects a social value."[2] The same can be said of ballads, and each form of folklore is intertwined within the folk culture.

For instance, among the twelve songs Big Daddy wrote down are two Civil War ballads. Several of the family anecdotes my aunt told me are also concerned with the Civil War and its aftermath. We are interested in the Civil War today in an historical way, but to people in Arkansas in 1907 it must have still been a vivid memory. My great-great-grandmother Faubus was a young woman during the Civil War and told stories about it to my aunt. "I can remember what an impression it made upon my mind as a child of the things she would tell us so terrible about the Civil War." She told of the time during the War when "bushwhackers" dragged her two-year-old child to death. My aunt recalled the story from her childhood. "She would tell that and we children would just sit and cry, and my mother used to say, 'Oh, I wish Grandma wouldn't tell you all these things.' It would just upset us."

Aunt Ocie told another story that took place when she was a baby which became a part of family tradition. The anecdote illustrates how the after effects of the Civil War were still being felt in Arkansas as late as 1910, and it also shows that Arkansas was in many ways still a frontier society at the time Big Daddy wrote the songs down.

When I was just a baby, my grandparents and all of the brothers—my daddy had, of course, these seven brothers, seven boys and three sisters—and the whole family had gone to church, a little country—it was just a meeting house for everybody. And these renegades from the Civil War were still just running wild and robbing; and they would come and rob people's smokehouses that had their meats or steal a cow or a calf and just butcher it right there. And we had gone to church, and during the service—now, I don't remember it because I wasn't but eighteen months old, but they told what happened. This group of renegades came, and they called and called, and wanted to disrupt the church service, and wanted them to come out. They didn't want any preaching in that part of the state, wasn't going to have any church in Arkansas.

So some of the boys went out and tried to talk to them, and they set up grindstones. Now if you know what that is, you know it has a big handle, and they sharpened knives out there and let it be heard inside—all, of course, an old log cabin—let it be heard all while the services were going on. So they prolonged it as long as they could and finally some of the boys came out and talked with them, and they would not listen to any talking.

Everybody wore a gun in those days, never went without a gun. Now Uncle Monroe was just real hot-headed, and if he'd had a gun that morning he would have gone out there and probably just shot the whole outfit of them. Do you know that not a single boy wore a gun to church that morning. They wore them all the time, but not a single one of those seven boys wore a gun to church that morning. So when they went out they just used anything in the world. They lit into them with these knives, and one of my daddy's brothers was just cut all the way down; his belt was the only thing that saved him. I don't know how many stitches they had to take in the end. And one of them started for me in the wagon, and my grandmother, my daddy's mother, took a water bucket, which was a big old wooden bucket, you know, with bails around it, and she took this water bucket and let this fella have it over the head with this water bucket when he climbed up in the wagon where I was. And they had to take him in and have so many stitches taken in his head.

And it was months later that some of the boys were in the barber shop, and this man was in there getting a hair cut, and he let out an oath that long, and he said, "Oh, be careful. That's where that Mullen woman laid my head open with the water bucket."

The story is exciting enough to become a part of family oral tradition, and it also adds a comic element at the end which makes it an even better story. It functions to perpetuate a sense of pride in the family by showing ancestors who are courageous in adverse situations. My aunt told me that it was a common occurrence in those times to have renegades attack the residents of the area.

In this rough society music created by the people was one of the few forms of entertainment. They sang secular and sacred songs. Of the twelve songs from 1907 only one has an explicit religious tone, but my aunt said the church and religious music played an important part in their lives. The family went to church every Sunday even if it meant having to leave on Saturday night to travel to a distant meeting place. They sang the "old hymns" in church and at home. My aunt recalled the ways the hymns were learned and sung. "They learned mostly by memory. I can even remember when I was a child of the one person standing up and reading a stanza and then everyone would join in and sing, and then he'd read the next stanza because books were, you know, just not too easily come by." This, of course, is the traditional "lining-out" method of singing hymns, still found in some rural churches today.

The secular songs that they sang in Arkansas in 1907 consisted of folk lyrics, popular songs from print, folk ballads, and play party songs. The settings for these songs can be discerned from family anecdotes; several of the family stories deal directly with the way old ballads were sung. There is one story which paints a warm and loving picture of Grandmother Faubus.

I as a child can remember when we would go to my grandmother's. She (Great-grandmother Faubus) would sit out against the smokehouse late in the evening and light a cob pipe and smoke, and all she would ever say—she would lean back in this old rawhide bottom chair—Grandpa always kept her a rawhide bottom chair—and she would lean back against the smokehouse and these old logs with the clay daubed in there. And she would sit there and hum old ballads, old songs, and every time she'd get through, she would say, "Ah-h-h-h Lordie." And that was just about the extent of her conversation.

This story also could be considered a type of local character anecdote, but often family stories concern themselves with the eccentricities of family members. The reference to the ballads is an important part of the narrative; the family anecdote reveals some of the context of the ballads.

Another anecdote from the family saga concerns the way in which Big Daddy sang folk songs to children.

He used to sing them, and he didn't rock us; as a matter of fact, he trotted us on his knee And he'd just trot and trot and hold you by the two little hands while he trotted. And he'd sing these ballads to us. And I don't know, they just really stuck with me through the years. I guess that's why I kept all of them.

This story functions to keep the memory of an individual alive within the family, but it also says a lot about how the songs functioned. My grandfather sang the songs mainly to entertain children as he grew older. Perhaps in his youth in Arkansas they were sung

at parties or during courtship, but after he was married and had
children and grandchildren the songs were performed for them. Big
Daddy sang the songs as long as the children were young enough to
"trot." He sang to all four of his own children, and I have a vague
memory of him trotting and singing to me and my younger brother
and sister when we were children.

Thus, Big Daddy kept these songs in oral tradition until his old
age. According to my aunt, he sang the songs from memory; he
never had to refer to the written texts in order to sing them. Then
why did he take the time and trouble to write them down in 1907?
I think one of the explanations can be found in folk tradition. It
was the custom to keep "ballad books" and albums in the 19th and
early 20th Century.[3] Even the way Big Daddy signed and dated
the ballads is probably traditional. One study of a 19th Century
ballad album indicates that the writer signed his name in the same
manner Big Daddy used.[4] The other explanation for writing the
songs down has to do with my grandfather's personality. When I
asked my aunt why he did it, she replied:

> I think probably more than anything else was the fact that this fit his person-
> ality, that everything he did he could remember, every date. He could tell you
> exactly where he was, what he did. Like, I have books that are little note
> books of all his activities through the years, where he worked, how much he
> made, how many hours a day he worked; and he could just tell you something
> right to the very day and year that it happened and so forth. And I think that's
> why that he had written these down.

He was a man concerned with detail and order, and all of the things
he kept a record of he considered to be of value. I think he definitely considered the songs valuable and worth preserving.

The two Civil War ballads would have been of special value to
him. The family stories point out the importance of the Civil War
in the minds of the people in 1907. My aunt commented on the
transmission of the Civil War ballads. "In all probability they were
handed down, you see, from my granddaddy or some of his brothers to my daddy." Thus, in one sense, the ballads are a part of
family tradition. The two Civil War ballads are "Dying Soldier"
(Laws A 14) and "The Charge of Confederatesburg" (Laws A 17),

both native American Ballads.[5] Vance Randolph has collected
variants of these ballads in the Ozarks; "The Dying Soldier" (#216)
was collected in 1928, and "That Last Fierce Charge" (#234) in
1941.[6] Because the way my grandfather wrote the songs down
was determined by the size of the paper and because the form he
used reveals nothing about how the songs were sung, I have put them
into stanzaic form with end rhymes for easier reading. The words in
brackets indicate ones which were missing in the manuscript.

DYING SOLDIER

The sun was sinking in the west and fell with lingering rays.
Through the shadows of a forest where a wounded soldier lay
Beneath the shadows of the palmettos beneath the sultry southern sky
Far away from his New England home they layed him down to die.

A group was gathered around him his comrades of the fight.
A tear stole down each manly cheek as they bade him a last good night.
One dear friend and companion was kneeling by his side
And strove to stanch his life blood, but it was in vain he tried.

He thought upon the future but his thoughts were all in vain
While from his loved companions the tears flowed down like rain.
"Comrades," spoke the dying soldier, "Comrades weep no more for me
I am crossing the dark river beyond where all is free.

"Come gather around me comrades I have something I would say.
I have a story I would tell you ere my life blood ebbs away.
Far away in loved New England in that dear old pine tree state
There is one who for my coming with a saddened heart will wait.

"A fair young girl my sister, my joy and my only pride,
My love and care from my boy hood for I have none on earth besides.
My mother she is sleeping beneath the church yard sod,
And its many a year since her spirit went home to god.

"My father he is sleeping beneath the dark blue sea
And I have no relation, there is only Nell and me.
But comrades I am dying I shall never see her more.
She will vainly wait my coming at our little cottage door.

"When our country was in danger and called for volunteers,
She threw her arms around my neck and bursting into tears,
Saying, 'Go my dearest brother, I cannot bid you stay,
But from our dear old homestead I will wait you day by day.

" 'Then go my dearest brother drive the traitors from our shore.
My heart it needs your presence but our country needs you more.'
But comrades I am dying I will never see her more,
She will vainly wait my coming at our cottage on the shore.

"Come gather close comrades listen to my dying prayer.
Who will be to her a brother, shield her with a brother's care?"
The soldiers spoke together like one voice it seemed to fall.
"We'll be to her a brother protect her one and all."

A shade of reddish brightness over his marble visage spread.
He gave one convulsion shudder and the soldier boy was dead.
By the banks of the Potomac they layed him down to rest
A saddle for his pillow and a gun across his breast.

                                        Written by Harrison Mullen
                                        1907

THE CHARGE OF CONFEDERATESBURG

It was just before the last [fierce] charge two soldiers drew the reins.
With partings words and touching hands alas might [never] meet again.
One had blue eyes and curly hair, just nineteen a month ago.
He had red on his cheeks and down on his chin, he was only a boy you know.

The other one was stern and true, his fate in this world was dim.
He only trusted the more in those who was all this world to him.
They had fought together in many a raid and rode for many a mile,
But never before had met their foe with so calm and peaceful smile.

They looked into each other's eyes with a horrible desperate doom,
And the dark stern man was the first to speak, "Oh! Charley my hour has come.
We will ride together up yonder's hill but you will ride back alone,
And promise a little trouble to take for me when I am gone.

"Upon my breast you will find a face; I will wear it in the fight,
With light blue eyes and curly hair, a face like the morning light.
Like the morning light was a love to me she gladdened my lonely life,
But little cared I for the frowns of fate since she promised to be my wife.

"Write to her, Charley, when I am dead; send back my fair fond face.
Tell her how I fought and how I fell, tell her my resting place.
Tell her my soul will wait for her on the border land between
The heavens and earth until I come, and it won't be long I mean."

Tears dimmed the blue eyes of the boy, his voice was low with pain.
"I will do my fighting comrade's bid if I ride back again,
But if I am slain and you ride back pray do as much for me.
My mother at home must hear the news, write to her tenderly.

"It was one by one she lost us all she buried [all her hus] band's sons and I was
    the [last to] her country's call.
She cheered and sent me on, she stays at home like a praying saint.
Her fond face white with war her heart will be broke
When she hears I am gone, but I will see her soon I know."

Just then the orders came to charge for an instance hand touched hand.
They answered I and on the road this undevoted band.
They charged right over the crest of the hill where the rebels with the shot an
    and shell
Fired rams of death on the toiling band and cheered them as they fell.

They turned with a horrible dying yell for the heights they could not gain,
And all that escaped from the rams of death rode slowly back again,
But among the slain on battle field lay the boy with the curly [hair,]
And the dark slim man that rode by his side lay dead [beside him] there.

So there is no one left to write to the blue eyed girl the last words her lover
    had said,
And the mother that waits for her boy at home she will but learn he is dead.
And will never know the last fond thoughts he sought to gladden her pain
Until she crosses the river of death and stands by his side again.

Written by Harrison Mullen
May, 2, 1907

The largest group of songs within the manuscripts were sentimental ballads. Each one has a definite emotion to express, and
in some cases the emotion almost overcomes the narrative element
so that technically they fall somewhere between the ballad and the
folk lyric, but the narrative is still strong enough to consider them
ballads. The most pervasive emotion expressed in this group is
sorrow over parting. This would conform with the frontier environment in which my grandfather lived. Often people left family and
friends back East when they came to settle in Arkansas. Two of the
ballads deal with separation in Ireland and Scotland, "Barney
McCoy" (Randolph #776), and "Bonnie Jean." Lines such as "I
am going far away, Nora darling," and "Though seas may divide
and the mountains so wide" emphasize the dominant emotion.
Since many of the Ozark settlers were originally from Ireland, Scotland, or England these songs would have wide appeal. Since the
songs are similar, I shall give just one as an example.

BARNEY McCOY

I am going far away, Nora darling,
Leaving such an angel far behind,
It would break my heart into
Which I fondly give to you
Living happy with you Barney McCoy.

       Chorus
Then come to my arms, Nora darling,
Bid your friends in dear old Ireland goodby.
Then its happy we will be
In the dear land of the free
Living happy with you Barney McCoy.

I would go with you, Barney darling,
But the reason why I told you of before.
It would break my mother's heart
If from her I'd have to part
And go roaming with you Barney McCoy.

I am going far away Nora darling
Just as sure as there's a god that I adore,

And remember what I say
That until the judgment day
You will never see your darling any more—Chorus

I would go with you Barney darling
If my mother and the rest of them was there,
For I know we would be blessed
In the dear land of the west
Living happy with you Barney McCoy.—Chorus

Written by Harrison Mullen
April, 29, 1907

The parting of lovers can come in many ways; one of the songs concerns the familiar ballad theme of death. In "Sunny Tennessee" (Randolph #810) the lovers are parted, and when the young man comes home he finds his sweetheart has died. This may express the fear of settlers who left lovers back home when they traveled to Arkansas.

On a morning bright and clear
To my old home I drew near
Just a village down in sunny Tennessee.
I was speeding on a train
That would bring my back again.
To my sweetheart that was waiting there for me.

It has been but a few short years
Since I kissed away her tears,
And I left her at my dear old mother's side,
And each day we've been apart
She grew nearer to my heart
Than the night I asked of her to be my bride.

Chorus
We could hear the darkies singing as she said farewell to me
Far across the fields of cotton my old homestead I could see
There the moon rose in it's glory
And I told the sweetest story
To the girl I loved in sunny Tennessee.

As the train drew up at las'
Old familiar scenes have passed,
And I kissed my mother at the station door,
And as old friends gathered round
Tears on every face I found,
But I missed the one that I'd been longing for.

Then I whispered mother dear
Where is Mary she's not here.
All the world seems sad and dreary comes to me,
When she pointed to a spot in the churchyard little lot,
Where my sweetheart sleeps in sunny Tennessee.

The most sentimental ballad of the ones my grandfather wrote down is the "The Blind Girl" (Randolph #724). I also found this song in collections from Missouri[7] and North Carolina.[8] This sentimental ballad must have held great appeal for folk communities all over the South.

THE BLIND GIRL

They say dear father that tonight you'll wed another bride,
That you will clasp her in your arms where my dear mother died.
That she will lean her graceful head upon your loving breast
Where she who now lies low in death in her last hours did rest.

They say her name is Mary too the name my mother bore.
Dear father is she good and true like the one you loved before?
And are her steps so soft and low her voice so meek and mild
And father will she love me too, your blind and helpless child.

Please father do not bid me come and greet your new maid Bride.
I could not greet her in the room where my dear mother died.
Her picture is hanging on the wall, her books are lying near
And there is the harp her fingers touched and there her vacant chair.

The chair where by I used to kneel and say my evening prayer.
Dear father, it would break my heart, I could not greet her there.
And as I cry my self to sleep as now I often do.
Then softly to my chamber creep my new mamma and you.

And bid her gently press a kiss upon my throbbing brow
Just as my dear old mamma did; Poppa you're weeping now.
I know I love you poppa dear but I have longed to go where
God is light and I am sure there'll be no blind ones there.

The prayer was offered and a song I'm weary now she said,
Her father raised her in his arms and laid her on the bed.
And as he turned to leave the room one joyful cry was given.
He turned and caught the last sweet smile, his blind child was in heaven.

They buried her by her mother's side and raised a marble fair.
On it inscribed these simple words, There'll be no blind ones there.

> Written by Harrison Mullen
> May, 1, 1907

One of the folk lyrics expresses a religious theme through a common folk song metaphor, the railroad. In Missouri, Belden discovered "various hymns or religious songs in which the process of salvation was presented under the figure of a railway train."[9] "Train Talk" is very similar to the traditional hymn "Life is Like a Mountain Railroad" also called "Life's Railway to Heaven."[10]

TRAIN TALK

Life is like a crooked railroad, and the engineer is brave
Who can make his trip successful from the cradle to the grave.
For he'll find enough obstructions ere his goal he'll safely gain.
On a curve, a fill or trestle when fate seeks to ditch his train.

But be mindful of instructions watchful duty never lack,
Keep your hand upon the throttle and your eye along the track.
Let faith be your conductor, hope your headlight in the night,
Let will be your strong fireman, and you're apt to pull through right.

You may run on grades and bridges full many a time with ease,
But some day you may be sidetracked by the switchman of disease.
But keep up the steam of courage, do not let hope's light go out.
Keep your fireman busy and you'll get back right no doubt.

In sorrows long dark tunnel keep your lights aglow with care;
Don't lose faith and jump off frightened, at the station of deep air.
Keep your hand upon the throttle, the sacred boon of breath.
Till you're to stop your engine by the signal-man of death.

Then you'll find with joy and comfort that you've reached your journeys end,
And the smiling superintendent bids you welcome as a friend.
Bids you enter His bright city in clean shining garments dressed
Where your railroads trials are oer you'll enjoy sweet peace and rest.

The other five songs illustrate the same general points I have been making. The broadside ballad "Rambling Boy" (Laws L 12)[11] condemns a life of sin and physical pleasures in keeping with the importance of religion in the lives of Ozark people. "Sady Ray" (Randolph #770) is a sentimental lyric ballad in which the dominant emotion is sorrow over the death of a sweetheart. "I Went My Love to See Her" deals sentimentally with false love. Two of the lyrics are popular written pieces which became part of the folk tradition in the Ozarks, "Hello Central" and "Absence Makes the Heart Grow Fonder."

Folk lyrics and ballads were a part of my grandfather's life and a part of the lives of the people of the Ozarks. Rather than present just the texts of the songs, I have tried to place them in the context of Arkansas society in 1907. One of the means of presenting context was the Mullen family anecdotes which sprang out of this period. The family stories present a more complete picture of what the songs meant then. A complete study of the folk culture would involve investigating the songs, the family stories, legends, folktales, superstitions, proverbs, riddles, folk crafts, and so forth. But relating together two genres of folklore from the same culture partially accomplishes the purpose of viewing folklore within its social context. All too often, family folklore is neglected as a source of cultural material, but it can be a valuable area of research by itself or combined with other genres. The result of studying folk songs within the context of family anecdotes indicates the value of examining cross-genre relationships in folklore.

NOTES

[1]Mody Boatright, "The Family Saga as a Form of Folklore," in *The Family Saga and Other Phases of American Folklore* (Urbana, Illinois, 1958).

[2]Boatright, 2.

[3]Harold W. Thompson and Edith E. Cutting, *A Pioneer Songster: Texts from the Stevens-Douglas Manuscript of Western New York, 1841-1856* (Ithaca, New York, 1958).

[4]Ruth Ann Musick, "The Old Album of William A. Larkin," *Journal of American Folklore, 60 (1947)*, 201-251.

[5]G. Malcolm Laws, Native American Balladry (Philadelphia, 1950).

[6]Vance Randolph, *Ozark Folksongs*, four volumes (Columbia, Missouri, 1949).

[7]H. M. Belden, *Ballads and Songs Collected by the Missouri Folk-Lore Society* (Columbus, Missouri, 1940, 1955), 275-276.

[8]*Frank C. Brown Collection of North Carolina Folklore*, six volumes (Durham, North Carolina, 1952-1965).

[9]Belden, 468.

[10]Ralph Rinzler, "The Greenbriar Boys," Vanguard LP VRS-9104, Vanguard Recording Society, New York.

[11]G. Malcolm Laws, *American Balladry from British Broadsides* (Philadelphia, 1957).

REVIVE US AGAIN

Joyce Gibson Roach

MY hometown has never been known for riotous living. It is a small community in north central Texas and, in my youth, somewhat isolated by distance and slow cars from the sinful city. School took up nine months of the year and that was looked upon as entertainment enough for most of us. It was every kid for himself in the summertime. My friends and I entertained ourselves with revivals, and judging from the numbers gathered as each church took its turn, lots of other folks took a certain pleasure in revivals too.

According to the thinking of the protestant churches, the members of their congregations had become lukewarm Christians during the winter months and inattentive to the Holy Spirit. Backsliding and grace falling, and general looseness in church doctrine was everywhere rampant. Only a round of loud gospel singing and hellfire preaching from someone strange, from a place at least thirty miles away, could set our feet on the path to glory. As an extra inducement, my church offered ice cream or watermelon in order to get the young people there for an extra hour of Bible drills and scripture memorizing.

I looked upon the first revival of each summer as a debutante looks forward to her coming out party. My family approached the season with fear and trembling. You see, revivals had a strange effect on me. I do not know whether it was the music, or the

65

preaching, or just a combination of things, but whatever the cause the results were the same. At the first call by the minister for re-dedication, I plunged down the aisle to give my heart anew to the Lord Jesus Christ, my Lord and Savior, and to whatever cause He had pending. Sometimes I gave myself to Christian nursing in the dark jungles of Africa; sometimes as a gospel singer in the slums of some big city like Breckenridge; sometimes as a missionary to the Indians in Arizona; and once to teach sewing to the poor little black children in my own community. Everybody knew I couldn't medicate, sedate, educate, sing, or sew a stitch, but I also believed in miracles. Every time the invitation was given my mother sat down. She knew what was coming. Sometimes others were struck by the same lightning, and we raced down the aisle to see who got there first to give their lives to whatever cause was hanging fire that evening.

But I'm leaving out the best part—the genesis of what went on before and led up to the exodus to the altar.

Things began for the young folks an hour before regular revival services. Mostly we had sword drills which commenced when the leader read out a scripture and then said, "go." You had to know the books of the Bible by heart and in proper sequence or you didn't have a chance to be first, unless of course they called a Psalm scripture. You could always find Psalms by opening the Bible as close to the middle as you could. The leader of the sword drills always threw in a Psalm or two to give the dunderheads a chance.

The sword drills were very hard on the Holy Bibles. Everyone would become so excited that very soon there were Bible pages lying all over the floor. The church must have felt that the drills were worth it because they always allocated funds in the budget for "Holy Bibles for sword drilling."

Sometimes after sword drilling, there would be a game called "Fill in a Scripture." The leader was invariably Sister Green who always began each season by "just lovin' us little ole children to death," and ended up the week by having a fit and telling our parents we were all going to hell—which had its redeeming features since Mrs. Green was bound for higher ground.

It was this game of "Fill in the Scripture" that stood her hair on

end and caused her to make such gloomy forecasts for us. The
parents never understood why she just didn't quit the game, but
she was stubborn. The problem about the game was that there was
no set, pat answer to her questions. You might answer with any
number of appropriate scriptures which you either knew or could
look up in your trusty sword drilling Bible. For instance, if she
said find a scripture about love, there was "God is Love," "God
loveth a cheerful giver," and "Love thy neighbor as thyself." But
there were other scriptures which someone always happened across
such as "Let him kiss me with the kisses of his mouth for thy love
is better than wine." (Solomon 1:2) We were off and running then.
And the more times we played the game, the more familiar we became with the "unusual" answers. She would move on faster and
faster. "Sports," she said. "Who can tell us about Bible sports?"
One kid jumped up. He was ready with "Genesis 26:8—Isaac was
sporting with Rebekah his wife." "Animals," she said, her voice
rising. Well, you know what animal everybody found, and I don't
mean donkeys. "Women," she shrieked. Sunshine Rowe replied
with a plum about whores, and Mrs. Green hit the door running
to tattle on us to our parents and everyone else who would listen
to her rantings. Sunshine shocked us all at the time, but he is in
the pen now, and I suppose Mrs. Green would think that only
justice.

There was a little time before regular services began, and we girls
would stand around in little clusters giggling and talking. The topic
of the house across the street usually came up, and that was good
for several minutes' speculation. The church ladies referred to it
as the house of ill repute. We didn't know what ill repute was. The
house did need paint and its two stories looked pretty spooky at
night. So a dark house in need of paint was what a house of ill repute meant to us. I particularly never connected anything very bad
with the place because I had a good friend living there. Minnie
Lake was her name. She bought Girl Scout cookies from me every
year and I made a pile out of that one house. I never told any of
the others where I did such a good business because I didn't want
anyone horning in. Nobody ever did. Mother knew of my acquain-
tance with Minnie. She never said anything about her, but she told
me never to go inside the house.

After we had visited a while, the crowd began to move on toward the arbor at the back of the church building. Choosing a fan was the next order of business. Fans served a multitude of congregational functions. Mothers fanned sleeping babies with them; men covered yawns behind them; ladies whispered behind them; some swatted flies and mosquitoes with them.

The first ones to gather got the best choice of the pictures. The fans were constructed of heavy cardboard with a stick glued on for a handle. The only funeral home in town distributed the fans to all the churches as advertisement. It seemed pointless except to remind you that the church and the funeral home would be with you at the end to take care of your soul and your body. Nowadays, the funeral homes don't pass out fans; they give away litter bags.

There were Bible or religious scenes on the cardboard faces of the fans. You could have one with an angel on it looking protectively down on two little children crossing a bridge above a raging torrent. There was one with Jesus knocking on a door. Another showed Jesus entering Jerusalem, and one had "The Last Supper" on it. My favorite, which I usually had to scuffle for, was Jesus praying in the Garden of Gethsemane. You could even see the sweat as drips of blood on his brow.

The schedule of events (I say events because that is what they often turned out to be) generally ran like this: the singing, the praying, the testifying, the edifying, the exhorting, the inviting, and the rededicating.

To get everybody quieted down, the song leader would tell us to open our paperbacked books, which we used for revivals because they weren't so expensive to replace when folks carried them off. Everybody enjoyed revival singing. We nearly always began with a chorus of "Hallelujah thine the glory,/ Hallelujah, Amen/ Hallelujah thine the glory,/ Revive us again." Then there would be songs like "Give Me That Old Time Religion," "At the Cross," and "Ivory Palaces"—if someone didn't sing it for a special. For the children they sang things like "I've Got the Joy, Joy, Joy, Joy Down In My Heart." Then at the end of the meeting we sang things like "Almost Persuaded" and "Just As I Am." There were more songs sung at a revival than at Sunday services.

After the singing came the praying, produced spontaneously by someone the preacher called on. Sometimes he would call on one of us older children to pray to show the parents how we were coming along in the prayer department.

There was always a special musical rendition after the praying and after more group singing. Usually there was a mixed quartet, and at least once during revival they sang what I called the question and answer song. The sopranos and altos would begin in harmony, "Who saved you from eternal loss?" On the word, loss, the basses and tenors would answer, "Who but God's son upon the cross." The ladies, on the word, cross, would sing, "What did He do?" The men answered, "He died for you." Building to a crescendo, the ladies trilled "Where is He now?" And the men boomed "Believe it thou." Then all would join for the final words, "In Heaven interceding." It was so pretty that most of the congregation joined in. We couldn't help it.

When the special music and the "Amens" which followed died away, we got ready for the testifying. The preacher planned ahead of time for one person to come to the front and start it, and then anyone the spirit moved arose to enumerate his past sins and his present cleanliness because Jesus had washed his sins away. We children never testified, of course, because we were too young to know about hard sinning, but we could tell from the testifying that we had a lot to look forward to.

After the testifying, and while the regular preacher introduced the visiting minister, the congregation made seating adjustments and prepared to settle down for the edifying.

The preacher had but one job and always the same job, to tell the gathered assembly in the most dramatic and stupefying way possible about sin—all the different kinds of sin, and how we were living in it, committing it, and could be saved from it. The style depended on the preacher, but it all came out with the gaiety of a Wagnerian opera. Fist pounding, hand clapping, finger snapping, and floor stomping were guaranteed to keep the attention and prove sincerity.

Those revival preachers spared the congregation nothing. They were far ahead of medical research in telling of the dangers of alcohol and tobacco. Dancing and swearing were dwelt upon with equal intensity. The emphasis then was a negative one, on not do-

ing rather than doing. Every morning I got up not drinking, swearing, smoking, or dancing, and knew what a wonderful Christian I
was being.

Sometime during the sermon, the visiting preacher invariably put
one hand on his hip and pointed pointedly at the house across the
street and named something else you weren't supposed to do. For
strangers, those visiting preachers always seemed well acquainted
with the town.

After the preacher had covered all the bases on sinning, he proceeded to the exhorting. That did not take long. He explained how
you would feel when the Holy Spirit hit you, and he begged you to
let it come upon you. Members of the congregation began to look
around now to see if the spirit was going to descend on anyone
they knew.

By the time the invitational hymn was beginning, some members
were already moving out to stand beside the worst sinners—teenage
boys, hardened husbands, and total strangers whose spiritual conditions were unknown and thereby constituted reason enough to
stand by just in case.

After three or four verses and a satisfactory amount of new material had been gathered at the altar, the preacher called for prayer
during which time he wanted "every head bowed and every eye
closed" while he made an appeal for Christians to rededicate their
lives to some specific or general cause which he named off. That
was my cue, and by the time every head was raised and every eye
opened, there I stood, to the joy of the strange minister, the dis-
gust of the congregation, and the shame of my parents. Afterwards
there was a lot of hand shaking and crying. Then we all went home
to rest up for another night.

We went just as joyfully to other revivals as we did to our own.
There was one church revival, however, I was forbidden to attend
regularly, and that was the Holiness meeting. Naturally I liked it
best. Whatever holy spirited-ness the other groups mustered, it was
clear that the Holiness had cornered the market. Everyone else
went to hear the speaking in tongues, which sounded like a lot of
lisping, and the hand clapping, and the floor rolling. I went to see
Jewanna Baxter, the preacher's daughter. She wasn't much older
than me but she had really lived, both religiously and otherwise.

Mrs. Smith, the town gossip and one of my dearest acquaintances, told that her daddy had included Jew in her name because they were God's chosen people and he wanted to get her on the bandwagon. She certainly had every right to make it—jet black hair and big brown eyes. She reminded me of Delilah, or rather of Hedy Lamar who played Delilah in the movie. She had her share of Samsons too, Jewanna did.

Jewanna could sing like a bird, but when she got to singing, and swaying, and praying, and pulling at her clothes my mother jerked me up and took me home. Ecumenicism went just so far with mother.

We never knew by any calendar date when the revivals were. Usually you met some friend and, when you asked her to play, she would look as if she'd just taken the veil and reply in tones dulcet and dignified, "No thank you. We are in a meeting." Then you hurried home and took a bath so you could beat her there. You might go to Heaven unwashed because no man knoweth the hour, but you didn't go dirty to a revival.

They say that all good things must come to an end, and so it came to pass that not summer revivals but my enthusiastic participation in them ceased. The cure was worse than my disease. It came about in this way. One prayer meeting night in late spring, the deacons met to plan for the coming revival in June. To stimulate interest and to show that we weren't backwoods Christians, which we really were, the deacons decided to invite what was then considered a new style evangelist, a professional revivalist. The board chairman announced that the man was of "foreign extraction," but he admonished us to remember that we are all brothers under the skin. The congregation thought the deacons had invited a black man, but, when they said his name was Juan Gonzales, we knew he was merely dark brown.

When Juan pulled up to the church in his red convertible wearing a red plaid jacket and accompanied by his blonde wife, the church members decided that there was a lot more to worry about than his foreign extraction. One fact was plain to see: he ought to really be able to tell us about the wages of sin because he looked as if he had seen some.

Juan's services were really something. Instead of the special music being sung, Juan blared it out on a trumpet while his wife accompanied him by knocking out a boogie beat on the piano. His preaching was different too. He didn't shout very much. Sometimes he whispered and hissed, and one time he actually cried. His sermons always mentioned hypocrisy, and, when he went into detail about the hypocritical disease, I knew that I had been an unsuspecting sufferer from it. There wouldn't be any more trips down the aisle for me. He would see right through me. When the call was given that night, I kept my place, and mother, instead of being overjoyed, put her arm around me. Juan had a strange effect on other people too. Many who had never gone down the aisle before stepped forward and did their duty.

Well, that's about all I remember about that revival when Juan came. I was sad and some wiser, and after that mother let me sit down close to the front by myself which she had never let me do before. I guess she knew that when the roll was called up yonder I might be there, but I'd sure think it over first.

CORRER DEL PAISANO

MR. McGovern owned a saloon at Kountze and Uncle Owen was a good customer. But Uncle Owen swore off and even went up to Dallas to take the Keeley Cure. (He said up there he was given all he wanted to drink while they were curing him . . . and there were chamber pots full of whiskey with gingersnaps floating around on top placed here and yonder all over the place.) Anyway, the first month after he got back, Mr. McGovern sent him a bill for six quarts of whiskey. Uncle Owen rode over to Kountze to see Mr. McGovern. He said, "McGovern, I haven't bought any liquor this month. I've even been up to Dallas and taken the Keeley Cure." "Well," said Mr. McGovern, "How was I to know? . . . It was here for you and if you didn't get it that was your fault." Uncle Owen studied about it a little while and then said, "Well, McGovern, if I'm gonna have to pay for it anyway, just wrap it up and I'll take it along."

Lois Williams Parker
Beaumont, Texas

PAISANOS AT ALPINE

Elton R. Miles

THEY like people and the fascinating things people do, say, and sing that they didn't learn in school. They love the Texas land, its wild flowers and prickly pear. They call themselves Paisanos, or fellow countrymen, and in the spring, they come together from academic towers, cotton farms, city streets, cattle ranches, and oil fields. They fetch their scholarly essays bristling with motif code numbers, guitars and banjos, tales about haunted stock tanks, recipes for poke salad, and curses for snakebite. They bring their gregariousness and their wives and children, and they muster for a meeting of the Texas Folklore Society.

Early in their careers the Paisanos liked to leave the meeting house and stretch their legs in some part of the communicative Texas land. In Austin in 1927 after a brief business session, automobiles carried fifty or seventy-five people to examine Indian Mounds being excavated under Professor J. D. Pearce's direction at Cedar Park. In 1939 Paisanos met at the San Jacinto battlefield, and in 1941 they assembled among the restored Mexican homes and shops of La Villita in San Antonio, where the program included a stroll along the river. While Austin and the University of Texas have always served as the TFS nerve-center, Paisanos divide their attention throughout the state. The third annual meeting in 1913 went to Waco where Dorothy Scarborough arranged for the Paul Quinn University Singers to demonstrate Negro folk songs. At San

Fifty-Second Annual Meeting of the Texas Folklore Society
Friday & Saturday, April 12 & 13, 1968, At Alpine
Host Institution: Sul Ross State College

Marcos in 1917 Paisanos observed a demonstration of folk dances of several different countries.

In 1926 the Society adopted the roadrunner as its emblem. In 1932 they urged the Texas Legislature to provide funds for the preservation of longhorn cattle, which may now be seen at the Fort Griffin State Park. Even during the two World Wars, when meetings were suspended, TFS affairs were kept in order. The meeting-less years were 1918-21 and 1943-45. That meeting in Denton in 1942, however, was covered by *Life* (June 1, 1942) with a large photograph of Paisanos swapping stories around an open fire.

Singing and swapping tales and traditions are forms of Paisano participation at the meetings. Members sling on their guitars, sing before the group, lead group singing, sing without accompaniment, tell tales, recite set speeches and poems, offer variant versions, and most of all unite in a celebration of their own lively folk heritage. Early meetings sometimes featured demonstrations of folk singing and folk dancing along with the papers, and by 1935 in Dallas more extensive group participation had started. At the dinner that spring each Paisano and guest told a story or presented a folk rhyme or expression, and, the record says that "it was the most delightful occasion ever experienced by any folklore gathering." In 1939 in Austin on the Student Union patio one of the first real hootenannies was held. At the dinner and on the patio Brownie McNeil played guitar and sang, Violet Sone and her daughter jumped rope and recited the rhymes, John Faulk and Boyce House told stories, Dan Storm fiddled, and there was square dancing for all.

The most memorable meeting of the past decade took place in Sul Ross State University in 1968. At least, Alpine was the head-quarters. The paper sessions were held in Big Bend National Park and in the Davis Mountains, and the members moved in caravan from one meeting site to another. Brownie McNeil, the University's president, was the host for the year, and he opened up the empty girl's dormitory for the Society. Everybody brought his own bedding and his own bar of soap. There was no scheduled hootenanny Thursday night, but Paisanos sang in the lounge and on the dormitory steps in the moonlight until long after most of them were in bed. Breakfast was at daybreak and then the group loaded into busses and cars for the scenic drive through mountains and desert

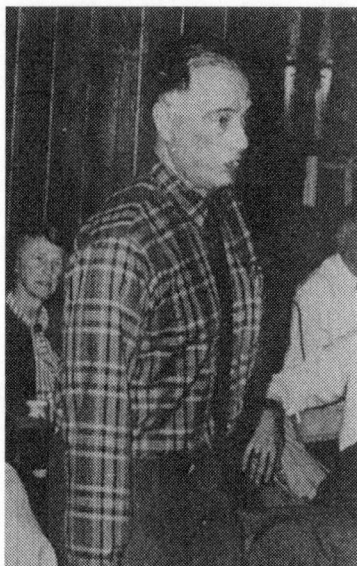

and across a flooded draw. After the rain the Chisos Mountains were studded with diamond-like points of light in the sunshine.

On a height overlooking the Rio Grande and the majestic Santa Elena Canyon, the first series of papers was presented. Afterwards, caterer trucks pulled up and served lunch. Busses and cars loaded again, and the Society moved on to the center of the Big Bend National Park, where more papers were read at the park's Campfire Circle. In one of the most significant items of business in TFS history, Mody C. Boatright was named Fellow of the Texas Folklore Society, in company with Leonidas W. Payne, John Lomax, and J. Frank Dobie. The final event of the night was a total eclipse of the moon that took place during the drive back to Alpine.

The Paisanos left early Saturday morning for the Davis Mountains State Park and that spectacular hill of mammoth boulders, the Rock Pile, for paper reading and the business session. As at the Campfire Circle the day before, children climbed mountains while their parents listened to papers and wondered where their children were. Already in place near this beautiful but unaccommodated Rock Pile were two sturdy pine booths, each with its sawed-out half-moon, one labeled "Paisanos," and the other "Paisanas." Right on schedule again came the food trucks, and after that a tour of the McDonald Observatory and Fort Davis National Historical Site, the restored army post dating from the 1850's for control of nomadic Indians.

The 1968 meeting of the Texas Folklore Society was formally concluded Saturday night with a Mexican banquet and an after-dinner hootenanny. Informally the Paisanos sang long into the night. Presumably they will be singing for many meetings to come.

FROM AMNESIA TO ILLEGITIMACY: THE SOAP OPERA AS CONTEMPORARY FOLKLORE

Sarah Greene

OPPORTUNITIES for the housewife to exchange gossip in our mobile, urbanized society are not what they were in those simpler times when women talked over the back fence as they hung out their wash or met in sewing circles and quilting bees. Chances now are that the housewife's next-door neighbor, whom she may hardly even know, is at work in the office or factory and even if Mrs. Housewife makes a weekly escape to the beauty shop she won't find it the fertile source of unauthenticated titillating information it once was. Into the gossip vacuum has rushed soap opera, an ersatz variety of life and art made available by the pervasive presence of the TV screen on the American scene. Soap opera has become a part of the customs, rituals, traditions, and beliefs of modern American folklore.

Programming of soap opera in the daytime hours has burgeoned from a modest beginning in 1952 into a cultural phenomenon that has molded a large segment of the populace into a community that cuts across socio-economic and racial lines. Residents of this Marshall McLuhanesque electronic village, whether the society matron and her Negro maid, or friends kept by geographical separation from meeting often, find common conversational ground through their interest in situations like the following—one that the local tale-spreader, no matter how long in the tongue, would be hard-pressed to match within the loose confines of reality that even the rankest gossip imposes:

Dr. Paul Stewart has leased his medical practice so he can go with his wife, Liz, to a sanitarium where she will be treated for a breakdown following her recent miscarriage. Liz desperately wanted the baby because she and Paul know that their young daughter, Betsy, is not his, since Liz was pregnant by another man at the time of their marriage. Neither Paul nor his doctor brother, Dan, knows that Betsy is Dan's child. The miscarriage was brought on when Dan's wife, Susan, convinced her husband's affair was still going on, threatened Liz that she would file for divorce, naming Liz as co-respondent.

Dan's real mother, Ellen, married his adoptive father, Dr. David Stewart, after the first Mrs. Stewart died and Ellen served a prison term for killing the housekeeper who threatened to tell Dan who his real mother was. Ellen's two daughters dug up an old picture album and told their great-grandfather, Judge Lowell, they had found a picture of Betsy. The judge, seeing it was really a baby picture of Ellen, in a blinding flash realized Betsy was Dan's child, Dan having confided to Judge Lowell about the affair. Judge Lowell has developed insomnia.

The judge's friend and law partner, Chris Hughes, and his wife, Nancy, have two of their three grown children living at home, Dr. Bob, whose two marriages have ended in divorce, and Penny, who lost the two husbands she loved to car accidents and divorced a third. Liz had spilled the truth about Betsy's paternity to Penny, who is wringing her hands because she was responsible for Liz's having come from England to make her home wtih the Hughes in the first place.

Lisa Shea, Dr. Bob's first wife, has been told by her ex-husband John Eldridge that she faces financial reverses because her investments are going sour but she has the Howard Hughes-type tycoon, Simon Gilbey, in view as a prospective fourth husband.

As any Faithful Viewer knows, this was how matters stood 4,000 episodes after the world first began to turn on CBS on April 2, 1956. On top of the ratings almost since its inception, the grand dame of the TV soap opera seems ever determined to prove Job's Biblical injunction that "man is born to trouble, as the sparks fly upward."

As the World Turns on a given day attracts 10,000,000 viewers, about 50 percent of the available audience, and daytime serials as a whole are seen by about 18,000,000 Americans. Luci Johnson Nugent and Van Cliburn are reported to be ATWT fans, and when Van visited the set in New York several years ago he confessed to an interviewer that he was probably hopelessly hooked, adding something to the effect that a person can't play the piano *all* the time. The intense involvement of viewers as they follow their favorite characters through familiar predicaments and worse makes the actors something more, in some cases, than equity card carriers. Four who seem well on their way to becoming folk figures are Nancy Hughes, Penny Wade, Lisa Shea, and Grandpa Hughes, all characters on *As the World Turns.*

A few years ago Neiman-Marcus advertised an expensive Sony portable TV set with the caption: "Haven't you always wanted to see Nancy's kitchen in color?" Faithful Viewers all knew that Nancy's kitchen is the folksy early American heart of the Hughes home, where Nancy dispenses coffee and sympathy and takes out her frustrations by kneading a loaf of homemade bread or whipping up, from scratch, a batch of cookies. Helen Wagner, the actress who portrays her, describes Nancy as a "tentpole character." Nothing ever happens to her, but she is all things to all people. Nancy finds her happiness within her home and herself, and she believes this is woman's true function. Women's Lib would turn her off, a characteristic she shares with virtually all female soap opera characters, even the dedicated lady doctors who are so much more numerous in soapland than in real life.

Lisa, "the girl you love to hate," has become so real to many that she has received threats on her life and was once slapped by an irate viewer outside her New York apartment. Eileen Fulton, who plays Lisa, says that though she has shown herself to be a liar, a cheat, a conniver, and a nymphomaniac, she loves her children more than anything in the world, so women forgive her. Indeed, it is a bit of Madison Avenue folklore that a woman soap character can operate outside conventional morality with impunity as long as she is a Good Mother.

Penny had been a popular figure through the 1960's. When the actress who portrayed her, Rosemary Prinz, wanted to pursue her career elsewhere, the writers shipped Penny off to England as they began to phase her out. In an interview with a Dallas newspaper, Miss Prinz reported that public pressure had demanded that Penny return. The new Penny, Phoebe Dorin, bears a strong physical resemblance to the old, a detail that is a sure indication of her importance. Though sponsor, producer and writer can banish a character, in the end the viewing audience can prevail by writing letters in scary enough numbers.

, As a popular figure must be retained, so must a villainous one get his just desserts, or Faithful Viewers will be heard from. Every woman in the viewing audience experienced the thrill of justice triumphant when a mysterious woman emerged out of Dr. Michael Shea's past and shot that shameless exploiter of women, who had driven Claire Cassen into alcoholism and Lisa Shea into temporary insanity.

Grandpa Hughes, who lives with Nancy and Chris, got 145,000 remembrances, including ties, socks, handkerchiefs, cookies and tobacco, when his birthday was observed on the program a few years ago. He serves as the perfect foil to Nancy, always philosophical when she is at her most emotional, and given to stereotyped aphorisms. Recently Penny confessed that what was bothering her was that "life goes on, in spite of what's happening to Liz and Paul."

Grandpa soothed: "That's the way it's meant to be. We've got to make every day the first day of the rest of our lives."

Intrinsically, soap opera barely qualifies as folklore because it is an art form (if one is free with the word "art") that is written by a known author at a known time and is unchanged between the writing and the production. On the other hand, this art form is concocted out of America's folk beliefs, customs, and attitudes. The characters themselves are representatives of modern folk heroes and types and are as indicative of America's aspirations and what we believe we are as the Horatio Alger type is indicative of what we believed we were. The doctors and lawyers and other professionals, in spite of their predicaments and pecadillos, represent in their ideals what middle-class America believes to be the standard codes and most exemplary ways of life. Upper-middle-class, soap-opera-watching America views that world as the desirable and achievable norm. Add to this the fact that listening and watching soap opera is a tradition that stretches back to radio and the thirties and you have a unifying custom and a traditional leveler that is as Americanizing as going to church. The prime function of folklore is to provide the social cement that welds a group of individuals into a like-minded community. Soap opera does this.

Such is the cultural leveling power of television that viewers of all ethnic groups and economic levels seem to identify with the soap opera characters, who are a remarkably undiversified lot. The stories are racially integrated, but along the usual Super-Negro mold favored by the prime-time series shows. Most of the male characters are professionals, doctors and lawyers predominantly, and few have names outside the Anglo-Saxon pattern of Banning, Rogers, Whitney, and the like. The leading series takes place in vaguely located Middle Western cities like Salem, Oakdale, and Monticello. The purpose is to achieve an American Anywhere in which the TV audience can easily recognize the characters as American Everymen.

My home county, Upshur, is one of those basically rural East Texas counties described by D. W. Meinig in his essay on cultural geography, *Imperial Texas,* as being essentially the western extension of the Old South, still a relatively stable bi-racial society, homogenous, conservative and fundamentalist, composed mainly of descendants of the same people who settled it more than a century ago, folks who are widely related and widely acquainted. The county seat, Gilmer, has fewer than 5,000 citizens, and the opportunity for real gossip to flourish remains greater than in more cosmopolitan areas. Yet my research indicates the soap opera is just as addictive there as elsewhere.

Generally, women I have interviewed tend to fall into three loose classes:

1. Those who watch because the soap opera's Pandora's box of troubles makes their own lives seem idyllic by comparison.
2. Those who carefully avoid tuning in because the soap sorrows seem all too reminiscent of their own.
3. High-minded, conscientious types who regard watching daytime TV as a self-indulgent waste of time, possibly a character defect. These occasionally acquire the habit despite themselves, but soothe their consciences by making sure they always have green stamps to paste up, darning or other handwork to do, peas to shell or some other constructive chore to accompany their viewing.

Men's attitudes may in general be typified by the reaction of a husband who, it was reported to me, picked up a letter from his wife's sister and questioned the last line, which read, "By the way, Ellen's pregnant." He responded with a brief expletive when his wife had to explain who Ellen was. Other husbands are given to adopting a superior and condescending attitude when they happen on to their wives and their friends when they are hashing over late developments.

But the fact is that men and children together comprise thirty percent of the national audience, and quite a few men will manfully own up to their secret vice. A Gilmer businessman and a deacon of his church who has watched the world turn for a decade told me he could hardly wait for Lisa to get her hooks into Simon Gilbey. "Boy," he said, "she's going to eat him up."

Many women seem not to realize that it's unnecessary to watch every day to follow the snail's-paced story lines. Dramatic high points are sure to be recapitulated. Nevertheless, a 1971 executive meeting of the Friends of the Upshur County Library was delayed by ten minutes because three of the six officers couldn't tear themselves away from a crucial episode in *Days of Our Lives.*

The commonest folk expression used between friends to describe their favorite serial is "the story" or "our story." Telephones ring all over town immediately after important developments, and this can lead to confusion. One Gilmer businesswoman, just back from lunch and *Days of Our Lives,* was in deep telephone communion with a friend, who was as baffled as she was at how Mickey Horton could much longer conceal from his wife his affair with his legal secretary. A fellow worker, whom I'll call Rose, was looking more and more interested. When the conversation ended the businesswoman told Rose: "That was soap opera. I don't really know anything *that* interesting that's going on around here." "Oh," said Rose, "I just thought you were as big a gossip as I am."

Another Gilmer woman cancelled her long-standing weekly beauty shop appointment and had her hair cut so she could tend to it herself after she realized, with some irritation, that the only gossip she heard at the shop was about the TV characters she could watch at home for free. The TV set in the shop is turned on continuously from 9:30 A.M. when *World Apart* comes on until 3:30 P.M. when *Somerset* goes off. The shop owner and another customer have a running argument over whether *Days of Our Lives* or *Love Is a*

Many-Splendored Thing is the better bet at 1:00 P.M., the owner so far having prevailed even at the risk of losing more business.

Women frequently spread the addiction to their friends, and to do so is not without peril. As the Chinese are said to be held accountable for a person whose life they have saved, so a person who passes on her habit may be held responsible for the derelictions of "the story's" characters. A Gilmer housewife, a pillar of the Church of Christ, now blames the friend who introduced her to *Days of Our Lives* when the soap people fall short, as they constantly do, of her moral standards.

Gossip about soapland's inhabitants regularly blends with, and often supercedes, the genuine article at bridge clubs, coffee sessions and hen parties. At a Christmas party in Gilmer one of the guests electrified the gathering with her pronouncement that Mickey Horton was a "self-righteous prig." It took a long discussion to settle it, but most agreed finally that her character analysis was correct.

Most involved of all, outside of the cooped-up young housewives, are the old women viewers. In Upshur County, as elsewhere, they dressed up for Dr. Bob Hughes' and Sandy McGuire's much-ballyhooed garden wedding, and they grieve when a favorite passes. A Gilmer widow, her family reports, mourned for two weeks when Dr. Doug Cassen of *As the World Turns* died suddenly, and refused to be consoled by the fact that he turned up the next week on *One Life to Live*. His widow, the elegant Claire Cassen, herself fatally struck down by a car, has been especially missed for her chic wardrobe.

Families have complained that matriarchs tolerate behavior from their TV favorites that they wouldn't countenance for one minute in a member of their own family. One such widow kept her daughter and son-in-law waiting for thirty minutes rather than break into her story to accept the handsome present they had brought.

Soap opera fans have created a market for a new type of magazine that follows the gossipy format of the movie magazines in giving the latest lowdowns on the actors' career developments, private lives, theatrical backgrounds, and fan clubs. Publications like *TV Dawn to Dusk, All Day TV, Afternoon TV,* and *Daytime TV* have appropriated the same style of star-struck awe with which the

movie magazines chronicle the doings, real and imagined, of their
famous and would-be famous subjects. They cater to the same idol-
hunger of the teen-age girl, and they offer her, for 50 cents plus
tax, the same blend of behind-the-scenes gossip, question and
answer columns, and pin-up pictures that have long been staple
fare in the movie journals. They also provide tips on how to spot
your favorite soap actor on the late, late show, list recent cast
changes, and faithfully report on a folk custom within the industry:
anniversary parties for the casts.

Many Faithful Viewers would not be caught under the hair dryer
with one of these magazines, because to them the actor really *is*
the person he portrays, just as, to many, Vivien Leigh really *was*
Scarlett O'Hara and Rhett Butler never could have lived and
breathed if there hadn't been a Clark Gable.

A Kingston, N. Y., viewer succinctly summed up how this comes
about in a complaining letter she wrote to *TV Guide* magazine:
"I watch *One Life to Live* every day," she explained. "When Joe
Riley was killed I was so upset I cried. My husband sat there and
laughed at me. He kept saying Joe was only a character on a show.
When one watches a show long enough, one tends to forget that."

The worst sin a beloved soap opera personality can commit is to
moonlight by doing commercials. What could be more disconcert-
ing than to see noble, self-sacrificing Dr. Bob Hughes living it up
in a poker game and touting Schlitz beer? Or to see Penny Wade,
who's had so much hard luck already, rummaging around in a station wagon and having to admit, "I forgot the Phillips?"

Resented, too, by Faithful Viewer is the dizzying succession of
actors who may fill a given role. If an act-of-God emergency arises,
such as a blizzard in suburban New York, an announcement is made
just before the scene is played that a temporary substitute will
appear that day. But if a key character leaves the cast and a new
performer picks up the role, no explanation is given. Carried to
ludicrous extremes, this has given rise to such situations as a woman
marrying a man one day and exchanging tender words with another
actor the next. But, as Roy Winsor, producer of *As the World
Turns,* explains, "Our faithful viewers are a breed apart. They
accept the ludicrous with the good because they believe." In what?
"In the story. Everybody loves a good story."

True enough, one might say, an articulation of the obvious. We know that Americans have always enjoyed tall tales and yarns that feature humor and exaggeration. Soap opera is rich in exaggeration. No one family, as one militant non-viewer expressed it, could have so many troubles—but it represents a perversion of the American folk tradition in its almost total lack of humor.

Actress Bethel Leslie, who became a writer for *The Secret Storm* after a well-rounded career on Broadway, in TV and the movies, dealt with the problem in a magazine interview. Her first daytime TV role had been in *Love of Life*.

"I enjoyed that," she recalled, "because it was a funny part. And they're few and far between on soaps. The character was a gas, really nuts, really fun. I would like to see more humor on these shows. No soap opera has ever left the air with a laugh. Let's face that. But you have to get some humor into it. Otherwise, it's *unrelenting*."

We may predict that she is fighting a losing battle, because it is apparently a deeply-rooted piece of televison folklore that though the housewife may watch the Mary Tyler Moore show at night, she wants a diet of unrelieved woe during the daytime.

Faithful Viewers expect, and are usually rewarded by, a certain stability in "their" story. They know there will always be long, pregnant pauses, accompanied by organ chords and soulful looks, at moments of high emotion; that there will be "little chats" over endless coffee to discuss "What's wrong?" and "How do you feel about . . . ?" They know Lisa will land on her feet and Ellen will suffer. The Carol Burnett show has needed only slightly to exaggerate these conventions to produce its comic parody, *As the Stomach Turns*.

"Continuing stories," as the producers like to call them, are directly descended, of course, from the radio soap operas that enjoyed their heyday in the 30's and 40's, and in turn traced their ancestry to the newspaper and magazine serials of the 19th and 20th centuries.

The relationship between novel-writing and soap-opera-writing has been pointed out by *ATWT* Producer Winsor, who calls the soaper "a never-ending novel."

Novelist Walker Percy is another who noticed the similarity. He disclosed to *Time* magazine that he watches *Days of Our Lives* during lunch at his home in Louisiana every day because of his fascination with the recurrence of themes. "All the men get amnesia and all the women get pregnant," he has observed, referring, no doubt, to the strange saga of Dr. Tommy Horton, who turned up in Salem years after his family had given him up for dead in the Korean War. He was still suffering from amnesia, plastic surgery performed in a Chinese prison camp having rendered him unrecognizable to his family. Through endless months of agonizing suspense, Faithful Viewers were gradually given hints about his true identity while Dr. Tommy fell in love with his sister, Marie. The Hortons found out Tommy was their son barely in time to prevent an incestuous marriage, and the shock of it all sent Marie to a nunnery. Mr. Percy said he is thinking of writing a novel about a man with "progressive amnesia," who he thinks might be the ideal fictional character.

Sophisticates such as Percy, unlike naive viewers, seem compelled to work out a rationale for their habit. Two Gilmer women claim to have found an intellectual challenge in keeping track of how *As the World Turns* and *Days of Our Lives* imitate each other, and in anticipating the plot convolutions. For starters, both Dr. David Stewart and Dr. Tom Horton have sons who are in love with the same woman; both daughters-in-law have produced children by the brother they're not married to; both stories have women characters whose maternal instincts have driven them to murder or into mental hospitals; problems with adoption and mother-daughter relationships have plagued both houses. The parallels can be traced until the mind boggles, my informants report, and they have concluded that *ATWT* retains its supremacy in ratings largely due to its edge from being one of only two of the seventeen TV soap operas still being telecast live.

No critic has suggested that the soaps are serious writing, and at least one, Marya Mannes, has bemoaned the waste of talented actors on material she regards as garbage.

Critics don't sell soap, of course, but they stung sponsors and producers during the mid-1960's with their complaints that the serials lacked relevance. Writers began to deal with a few prickly and daring themes—drug abuse, homosexuality in prisons, ghetto

problems—knowing full well that they would dismay elderly followers conditioned to the familiar cries of the old "John! Marcia!"
genre. By 1970 it appeared that all taboos save one had fallen like
ripe persimmons: a doctor might get roaring drunk, but he would
never be seen smoking a cigarette. A far cry it was from radio
days, when the industry held the fixed belief that the housewife
was interested in no more sophisticated a social question than
"whether a girl from a mining town in the West can find happiness
as the wife of a wealthy and titled Englishman," and that she insist-
ed on soap opera characters being as pure as Ivory Snow.

But still the real-world social problems encountered most often
were mental illness, crime and traffic deaths. One had sadly to
assume that this was not due so much to any sincere interest by
networks and sponsors in combatting these plagues, but was rather
because of the fact that breakdowns, murders and car wrecks
serve the story lines so well, and provide an easy out when an
actor finds the $20,000- to $50,000-a-year grind of the soaps has
begun to pall.

The writers may sometimes overdo it a bit, a letter from a North
Carolina viewer to *Afternoon TV* indicates:

"I agree with the woman who wrote in and said *Days of Our Lives* is one of
the most well written shows on soaps today. The cast fight their problems
with every strength in their body, and when the going gets rough, which is
most of the time, they don't break down and get amnesia.

(She must have forgotten about Tommy Horton.)

"I really like a show when the people are emotionally involved and are determined to cope with the problems of every day life. When a person gets amnesia and the story gets boring, most of the time I start looking at another
soap."

Catharsis by comparison with others worse off, vicarious experience for those whose own lives are lacking in drama, voyeurism,
masochism, escapism—all these the TV hucksters are peddling. What
subtle transformations this fantasy world may be working on viewers of all ages remains unknown. Certainly the young, if lacking

in other resources, can find in the soap opera a new medium for sex education.

It may be argued that the stories serve as a sort of TV Dear Abby for the psychologically afflicted, or that they dispense their own brand of hope. On soap opera there is always tomorrow, fraught with problems, tragedies, and trauma. Life, on the other hand, also has a lighter side, and if we can rarely discern this from watching "the story," we can be grateful that since the tendency to gossip seems to be ineradicable in humans, at least when it deals with soap opera personalities no real lives are damaged.

Alice Horton, the "tentpole character" of *Days of Our Lives,* posed the crucial question when, surveying her family's rising sea of troubles, she lamented: "When will it end? Oh, when will it ever end?"

The cynic might reply that it won't end at all as long as NBC and the sponsors are satisfied with the ratings.

Faithful Viewer, true believer that she is, knows better.

CORRER DEL PAISANO

SALLY and nephew Lee had a religious argument. It was a matter of interpretation of the chapter and neither convinced the other, but they argued good-naturedly until past midnight when Aunt Sal finally lost her temper, blessed Lee out and took off to bed. But sleep failed to come to Sally. She had never meant to lose her temper. She prayed for forgiveness until along toward 4:00 A.M. when she decided to get up and make a pot of coffee. About 4:30 Lee heard a knock on his door. It was Aunt Sal with a cup of coffee in one hand and a washbowl full of water in the other. "Sit there on the side of the bed, Lee, and drink this coffee while I wash your feet, you old rascal," she commanded. Lee obediently sat while Aunt Sal went through the process of washing his feet. Neither spoke, but when she had finished, Lee leaned forward and kissed her. She left the room, took a long nap and the incident was never mentioned again.

Lois Williams Parker
Beaumont, Texas

MORE OF THE WORD ON THE BRAZOS

J. Mason Brewer

PLENTY H. JOHNSON'S CONCLUSION

ONE o' de bestes' Nigguh good-livers Ah done evuh seen't, or heer'd tell ob in mah whole bawn life was a Nigguh rat heah in Hearne, what go by de name ob Plenty H. Johnson. De why comed by dis heah name, so dey say, was 'caze he hab plenty o' evuhthingg—plenty money in de bank, plenty mules, plenty hosses an' cows in his stable, an' plenty pigs in his hawg pen. 'Sides dese heahs an' dem dars, he hab plenty grub in his smoke-house fer him an' 'is wife Mamie Lou, tuh sop on, an' smack on.

But Plenty ain't all us'; he putty nigh white folks wid long stringy black hair, an' he ain't low-lifed lack de rest on us what lib in us's li'l' ole shot-gun shacks long side de railroad track—he hab him a big sebun room crate on de white folks side o' town. His wife Mamie Lou ain't all us' neithuh, an' she a gawky yalluh 'oman wid 'er hair hangin' down 'er back way pas' her wais'. De why dat Plenty comed up in the worl' so fas' was dat he turned out tuh be de bes' cotton sampler in Hearne, down to de Hearne cotton compress whar he made de day, an' drawed his pay'; dey paid 'im top wages fer 'is wuck down dere.

But one time when day hab a long time drouf 'roun' Hearne,

'count o' Gawd gettin' tahd o' folks tryin' a monkey wid 'is bizniss an' shettin' up de Heabuns fer three yeahs an' not lettin' hit rain, cotton 'roun' heah was ez scarce ez hen teeth in Georgia, so de Hearne cotton compress whar Plenty wucked hab to close down. Of a consequence Plenty was lef' wid his livin' cut off.

De same mawnin' dat dey done tol' Plenty dey did'n hab no mo' need fer 'im he tuck his lunch bucket an' staa'ted back home in a deep study, 'caze he wonder, now dat he come out on de short end ob de horn, how he gonna tough hit out wid no money rollin' in. But he don' have de wisdom tuh know dat a white man fum Houston don' heer'd 'bout what a good cotton sampler he be an' was edgein' Hearne dat ver' minnit wid 'is hoss an' buggy on de way tuh Plenty's house.

W'en de white man driv up tuh Plenty's house, Plenty done already rech dere an' him an' Mamie Lou was settin' on de gall'ry jes' a hee-hawin' wid one nothuh. So de white man jumped outen his buggy, runned up to whar Plenty an' Mamie Lou was settin', an' ast Plenty am he Plenty H. Johnson. Plenty say, "Yas, Suh Ah ain't nothin' else but," so de white man ast 'im don' he wanna come down tuh Houston an' sample cotton fer 'im. He say he'll gib 'im twenny dolluhs a day. Plenty ain't nevuh heer'd tell of meckin' dat much money in a day in all his whole bawn life, so he don' hem an' haw 'bout de deal one way t'uthuh; he gee-haws rat now an' tell de man sho he'll teck de job. So de man tell 'im awright, he'll gib 'im a week tuh git his bizniss straight in Hearne 'fo' he show up in Houston fer wuck, an' he goes on out an' gits in his buggy an' drives on off.

W'en de end ob de week roll 'roun' Plenty an' Mamie Lou piled all dey b'longin's in dey wagon, feasted dey eyes fer de las' time on de fine crate whar dey been livin' fer de pas' twenny yeahs, an' driv on down tuh Houston.

So dat nex' comin' Monday mawnin' attuh Plenty done rech Houston he showed up at de white man's place o' bizniss an' tell 'im dat he am ready tuh go tuh wuck. De white man tell 'im dat he sho am glad tuh heah dat an' dat he wan' 'im tuh wuck all sebun days in de week includin' on Sundays.

Plenty keep tab on what de man say 'bout wuckin' on a Sunday, an' he almost' hab a change of haa't 'bout wuckin' fer 'im. 'caze he

been a deacon in de St. James Baptis' Chu'ch in Hearne fer de las'
pas' twenny-five yeahs, an' he don' b'lieve in wuckin' on a Sunday.
He 'low dat if'n you wucks on Sundays you'se goin' tuh Hell haid
fo' mos', an' dat dey ought to be a law 'ginst wuckin' on a Sundays,
so he tecks de white man to tas' an' tell 'im if'n he have tuh wuck
on a Sundays, he gonna hab to change his mind 'bout wuckin' fer
'im an' go on back to Hearne, 'caze he don' wanna go tuh Hell.
He say he wanna go tuh Heabun w'en he die.

So de white man tell 'im awright, dat he ain't nevuh let nobody
off fum wuckin' on a Sundays befo' but he'll do hit fer Plenty,
since he's sich a good han'. Plenty says, "Sho thanks yuh, Suh," an'
dat nex' Sunday comin' he goes down and jines de bigges' Baptis'
Chu'ch in Houston, what was havin' a rally tuh buil' 'em a new
chu'ch house. An' you know sump'n—dat ver' fus' Sunday dat
Plenty done jined up wid de chu'ch de pastor hist hisse'f outen de
pulpit rat attuh de servus an' say, "Now, brothuhs an' sistuhs,
Ah wants all o' y'all tuh come up tuh de colleckshun plate an' lay
a twenny dolluh bill down on hit tuh buil' de new chu'ch house."
Plenty hab a knack ob allus doin' what all de othuh membuhs in
his chu'ch do, so he do jes' lack de othuh membuhs in dis heah
chu'ch do; he walk up tuh de table an' plank a twenny dolluh
bill down in de colleckshun plate. De pastuh ob de chu'ch whar
Plenty done jined up do dis heah same trick fer five Sundays
straight; he ast all de membuhs tuh come up tuh de table an' lay
a twenny dolluh bill down on hit tuh hope buil' de new chu'ch
house. So Plenty yit do lack de res' ob 'em—walk up tuh de colleckshun table evuh Sunday an' plank down a twenny dolluh bill
down on hit.

But dat nex' comin' Monday mawnin', attuh de fifth Sunday
done swung by, Plenty walks ovuh tuh whar his boss-man am
stannin' an' asts 'im kin he pas' de time ob day wid 'im jes' a
minnit, an' de boss-man tell 'im sho he kin, so Plenty say, "Ah
don' want much of nothin'; Ah jes' wants tuh ast you if'n Ah kin
sta'at wuckin' on a Sundays lack evuh body else do."

"Sta'at wuckin' on a Sundays lack evuh body else do?" 'low de
boss-man. "Ah thought you done tole me when you tuck dis job
dat you did'n wanna wuck on a Sundays—dat you'd go tuh Hell if'n
you wucked on a Sundays."

"Yas, suh, Ah knows Ah did," 'low Plenty, hangin' his head down, 'caze he so shamed hisse'f. "Dat is what Ah thunk when Ah was up in Hearne, but since Ah's been down heah in Houston Ah's done foun' out dat hit's a whole lots cheaper tuh go tuh Hell dan hit is tuh go tuh Heabun."

LITTLE SAMMY & THE PRESIDING ELDER

Ah calls tuh min', down to Ole Washington on de Brazos, a croppuh what go by de name of Tom Brown. Tom was a trustee down tuh de school rat attuh de white folks' guv'ment builted a new cullud schoolhouse at Ole Washington, an' we comed to hab some putty good book-learnin'.

Tom hab a rat smaa't size li'l' ole eight yeah ole boy name Sammy, what was smaa't ez a whip, an' w'en de white folks' guv'ment builted de new schoolhouse an' hired a putty li'l' school teachuh from 'way somewhar tuh teach de school, Sammy comed tuh be teachuh's pet. Come to think of it, Sammy was de teachuh's stan'by in her Sunday-School class she teached evuh Sunday, too, 'caze t'othuh li'l' ole chilluns looked up tuh Sammy an' do what someevuh he do. He de leaduh of de bunch, so dat's de why de teachuh picks Sammy ez her pet, 'caze she kin rule all t'othuh li'l' chilluns thoo him. De teachuh teached de Primary Sunday-School class, an' she allus hab her class stay tuh lebun o'clock preachin' servuses, 'caze she done promus' de Presidin' Elduh ob de districk, Revun Williams, what fetch de teachin' job fer her, dat she ain't gonna be no suit-case teachuh, what grab up his suitcase full o' clo'es evuh Friday evenin' de Lawd see an' lope off home 'way somewhars an' don' come back tuh de Bottoms 'til on a Monday mawnin'. De teachuh, what go by de name ob Miz Jackson, 'low she gonna be paa't an' passel of Ole Washington lack evuh-body else be. She meck good her promus' too, an' comed up moughty quick ez a Sunday-School teachuh. Ebun de preachuh an' de ole folks 'low dat Miz Jackson was de cream of de Sunday-School teachin' crop dey's got at St. Andrews Mefdis' Chu'ch, what was way down by a putty patch ob timber in a moat, rat close tuh de schoolhouse. So Miz Jackson done got off tuh a good runnin' staa't, ebun if'n she do hab a rat smaa't crop of yaps tuh handle durin' de week-a-days. She don' only gee-haw rail good wid de li'l' ole chilluns, but hitches hosses wid de pappys and mammys lackwise.

Miz Jackson rat proud of herse'f, an' she can't haa'dly wait 'til de presiding elduh's time come tuh hol' his quart'ly con'funce at Ole Washington so he kin see for hisse'f how she keepin' her promus' 'bout workin' in de chu'ch an' not bein' no suitcase teachuh. She ain't gonna haftuh wait too long neithuh, 'caze de Friday fo' de fuss Sunday in Decembuh jes' fo' hog-killin' time, when she was walkin' down de lane comin' to'ads her on his ole roan saddle hoss but de pastah, Revun Burton. Revun Burton stop his hoss rat in his tracks, an' tell Miz Jackson dat Revun Williams gonna hol' his quart'ly meetin' at de St. Andrews chu'ch dat comin' Sunday an' tuh be sho an' hab her Sunday-School class stay fo' de lebun o'clock servuses. He say he goin' tuh ferry Revun Williams' cross de rivuh rat now, 'caze he comin' from t'othuh side ob de Brazos.

Miz Jackson jes' had a too'f yanked out dat mawnin' an' she ain't feelin' so pert, but she cain't in no wise miss dis heah Sunday, so she meets her Sunday-School class ez usual, an' aftuh Sunday-School done let out, she tecks all her li'l' Sunday-School scholars an' lines 'em up on a bench 'side her. She puts li'l' Sammy rat nex' to her so's she kin keep a watch on him and keep him wake durin' the sermon, 'caze she knows if'n she keep dis li'l' rascal wake all de res' ob de li'l' yaps gonna stay wake lackwise, an' Revun Williams gonna see how good she keepin' her promus' 'bout bein' a good chu'ch wuckuh.

No sooner'n Miz Jackson done lined up her li'l' Sunday-School scholars in comed Revun Williams an' Rev Burton an' sets down in de pulpit. Dey riz up a song, prayed, an' read outen de "Word," an' putty soon Revun Williams gits up, clears his th'oat rail loud, an' say, "Brothuhs an' sistuhs, de fuss thing Ah'm gonna tell y'all dis mawnin' am how tuh meck yo' COMPERACITY GASHIATE." He keep on talkin' in dis heah wise, usin' outlandish words dat nobody don' unnuhstan's 'til li'l' Sammy doze off to sleep. Leastwise Miz Jackson think he done gone to sleep, so she tecks her pencil outen her purse an' raps li'l' Sammy ovuh de haid to rouse him. Li'l' Sammy riz up his haid an' open his eyes, an' all to'othuh li'l' yaps settin' on de row wid 'im in de Primary Class do's lackwise.

No sooner'n Revun Williams staa't on de secon' paa't of his sermon an' say "Brothuhs an' sistuhs, de secon' thing Ah'm gonna tell ya'll how tuh do is tuh meck yo' CORPORATE GRADUATE, Li'l' Sammy bows his haid an' shuts his eyes lack ez befo', an' Miz Jackson gits so opset she don' know what tuh do wid herse'f, 'caze Li'l' Sammy done meck things go hay-wire again by dozin' off tuh sleep an' all t'othuh li'l' yaps in de Primary Class do lackwise, so she tecks her pencil outen her purse lack ez befo', an' whams li'l' Sammy ovuh de haid agin. Li'l' Sammy don' relish bein' hit on de haid, so he riz up his haid, an' open up his eyes, lack ez befo'.

He stay awake 'til Revun Williams tears out on de third paa't ob his sermon an' say, "Now, brothuhs an' sistuhs, de third thing Ah'm gonna tell ya'll how tuh do is how tuh meck yo' SATURATE ELUCIDATE; an' w'en he talk in dis heah wise, li'l' Sammy shuts his eyes an' bows his haid jes' lack befo', so Miz Jackson tecks out her pencil an' whacks li'l' Sammy ovuh de haid rail ha'ad dis time, but li'l' Sammy don' jes' open up his eyes an' hist up his haid dis time. He looks up at Miz Jackson rail pitiful lack, an' say, "Hit me a li'l' haa'duh, Teachuh, 'caze Ah still heahs him."

REVEREND BAILEY'S WATCH CHAIN

Rat attuh de Numbuh One Worl' War done come tuh a close, dey hired a uppity preachuh from waysomewhars to pastuh one o' de chu'chs down tuh Calvert. Dis dicty preachuh go by de name of Revun Bailey, an' he a reg'luh fashun plate in his dressin'. He allus wore a gol' watch chain in his ves', an' de chain hab a lots ob pins hangin' on it wid lots o' diffrent colors an' all kin's of things on 'em. Evuhbody look at de pins an' don' nobody know what de things on de pins stan' fo', 'caze dey ain't de square an' de level of de Masonics, an' dey ain't de han' shake of de UBF Lodge.

Evuhbody was in a wonduh ez tuh what dese pins stan' fer, but hit lef' up tuh Ole Man Johnson, a rail ole carpenter 'roun' Calvert tuh fix Revun Bailey's bizniss good. Once't Ole Man Johnson was buildin' a bawn on one of Revun Bailey's membuh's fawms, Tobe Allen's fawm, an' Revun Bailey come prowlin' 'roun' whar Ole

Man Johnson buildin' de bawn, an' showin' off de putty pins what
he got on his watch chain. Revun Bailey keep on fumblin' wid
de pins 'til fin'ly Ole Man Johnson say, "Revun, youse sho got
lots of putty pins on dat watch chain of your'n. What do all dem
pins stan' fer?"

"Well, Ah tells you, Brothuh Johnson," 'low Revun Bailey, "dem
pins means dat Ah knows evuhthing. See dis un rat heah; hit
means dat Ah is got mah A. B. from Fist Univus'ty; dis un on de
bottom means dat Ah's got mah B. D. from Gammon Sem'nary,
an' dis un in de middle ob de chain means dat Ah's got mah A. M.
from Linkum Univus'ty."

"Well, dat's jes' scrumptous, Elduh," 'low Ole Man Johnson;
"hit sho mus' meck a man feel good to know evuhthing, an' while
Ah thinks of hit, would you min' goin' ovuh dere tuh dat barrel
by de wadduh pump an' fetchin' me a han'ful ob ten-penny nails,
so's Ah kin finish nailin' up dis plank?"

"Naw, Ah sho wouldn'," 'low Elduh Bailey, so he moseys on ovuh
tuh de barrel what got de nails in hit, grabs up a han'ful o' nails,
an' brings 'em tuh Ole Man Johnson. Ole Man Johnson tuck de
nails, looked at 'em rail haa'd, an' den turnt tuh Revun Bailey an'
say, "Revun, dese ain't no ten-penny nails; dese heah's shingle
nails." Den turnin' tuh whar Tobe Allen's li'l' ole six yeah ole
boy Bobby was stannin' lookin' at 'im buildin' de bawn, Ole Man
Johnson say, "Bobby, run ovuh dere tuh dat barrel by de wadduh
pump an' bring me a han'ful of ten-penny nails." So li'l' Bobby
say, "Yassuh," an' goes on ovuh tuh de barrel an' fetches Ole
Man Johnson a han'ful of ten-penny nails lack he done ast 'im tuh
do; an' when de li'l' boy do dis, Ole Man Johnson turnt tuh Revun
Bailey, an' say, "Revun, Ah thought you know'd evuhthing; but
dis heah li'l' ole six yeah ole boy know mo'n you do. You don'
ebun know a ten-penny nail from a shingle nail." Dat's when people
staa't to doubt dat Revun Bailey know evuhthing.

THE UPPITY PREACHER & THE WARDEN

"People oughta count de cos' 'fo' dey staa'ts out; dey mought
haftuh pay too deah for things. Mah Papa allus tol' me dat a
bought whip was de bes' whip in de worl', if'n you didn' haftuh

pay tuh deah fer hit, but Elduh Bailey haftuh pay rail deah fer
de whip he done bought. He got so biggity in de chu'ch 'til he
staa't to mistreatin' de membuhs an' doin evuhthing unnuh Gawd's
sun wrong dat he feel lack doin', jes' runnin' 'way wid things. But
whar he slip up was w'en he sol' de chu'ch house organ tuh two
diffrent music sto's, an' dey 'rests 'im an' sen's 'im down tuh de
Huntsville Penitentiary. De fuss day he gits dere, an' dey sen's 'im
out tuh de prison fawm wid t'othuh convicts tuh pick cotton, an
de Warden walks up tuh 'im an' say, "Revun, Ah wants five hunnud poun's of cotton outen you today, does you unnuhstan'?"

"Yassuh, Ah unnuhstan's," 'low Revun Bailey, "Ah'll git hit if'n
de Lawd's willin'."

So dat same day, way late down in de evenin' time when hit
come tuh be weighin' in time, Revun Bailey brung his drag-sack up
tuh de wagon an' put hit on de scales, but dey wasn' but fifty
poun's in de whole drag.

W'en de Warden weighed Revun Bailey in an' foun' out he ain't
brung in but a fifty-poun' drag, he looked at 'im rail mean lack
an' say, "Revun, Ah done said Ah wanted you tuh hab five hunnud
poun's of cotton in yo' sack at weighin' in time. Now, Ah's gonna
gib you one mo' chance. Tomorruh, you bettah hab five hunnud
poun's of cotton picked by weighin' in time, o' you gonna rue de
day."

Howsomeevuh, Revun Bailey say jes' lack he do de day befo',
"Ah'll git hit if'n de Lawd is willin'."

So de nex' evenin' w'en weighin' in time roll 'roun' an' Elduh
Bailey brung his sack to be weighed in, he didn' hab no mo'n fifty
poun's in his drag sack again, so de Warden called t'othuh convicts an' say, "Boys, Revun here don' seem to unnuhstan' me w'en
Ah tells 'im Ah wants 'im tuh bring me five hunnud poun's of
cotton, so Ah speck y'all'd bettuh light in on 'im an' show 'im
what Ah means." So de convicts lays hol' on Revun Bailey an'
beats 'im up good-fashion, an' w'en dey done fix his bizniss good,
an' turnt 'im loose, de Warden walks ovuh tuh whar Revun Bailey
wipin' de blood offen his back, an' say, "Revun, does you unnuhstan' me now w'en Ah says Ah wants you tuh bring me five hunnud
poun's of cotton in by weighin' in time?"

"Yassuh, Yassuh!" yell Elduh Bailey, rail quick, jes' a pantin' an' a tremblin', "Ah unnuhstan's you now; Ah'll git hit if'n hits dere."

An' what you reckon? Well, dis is what dey say. Dat nex' comin' day, Elduh Bailey picked a thousan' poun's o' cotton wid one of his legs staked tuh de wagon wheel, an' de nex' day attuh dat un, he picked a whole bale by hiss'f.

At leas', dats what dey says in Huntsville.

DEACON JACKSON TAKES A NAP

You know de Baptis' don' lack dat condishun "Go!" De Baptis' preachuh sho'nuff falls down on dis sco' ob de Word. You know de Word say, "Go into all de worl' an' preach de Gospel," but de Baptis' preachuh stay one place so long 'til he kill hisse'f wid de membuhship. De membuhship git tiahed ob de same preachuh all de time, so ob occasion dey hab a split an' de ole pastuh ca'ies off a bunch of membuhs an' organizes a new chu'ch.

Ah calls tuh min' a Baptis' preachuh by de name of Elduh Bell, what pastuh de Baptis' chu'ch down tuh Childton. He done stay dere so long 'til de membuhship done slack dey intrus' in de chu'ch. He done preach de same sermons so long 'til de membuhs tiahed of lissunin' tuh 'im. Some ob de deacons wan' de pastuh tuh go 'way somewhar outen de Bottoms, 'caze lots ob de membuhs ob de chu'ch done lef' an' jined de chu'ch down tuh Jerusalem, but Elduh Bell hab mos' ob de deacons on his side, an' he don' quit. One ob dese deacons what don' relish 'im stayin' on was name Deacon Hunter; he say dat de chu'ch mean mo'n de man anywhars.

So fin'ly, one time, on a Sunday night in de mont' of August, w'en hit was pow'ful hot in de chu'ch house, an' Elduh Bell was a-preachin', an' sweatin' an' a-wipin' 'is face wid a hankershuf, he looked down an' seed Brothuh Jackson, one ob de deacons, done gone tuh sleep; so he stop preachin' in de middle ob his sermon an' yell out tuh Deacon Hunter, de deacon what don' relish 'im stayin' at de chu'ch, tuh wake up Brothuh Jackson, an' when he say dis, Deacon Hunter eyed 'im rail mean lack an' say, "Wake 'im up yo'se'f; you put 'im tuh sleep."

FROM FOLK TO HILLBILLY TO COUNTRY: THE COMING OF AGE OF AMERICA'S RURAL MUSIC

Bill C. Malone

THAT country music is a well-entrenched, vibrant, and lucrative facet of American popular culture is a fact that need no longer be documented. The wide appeal demonstrated by the Johnny Cash, Glen Campbell, and "Hee Haw" television shows reminds us that rustic entertainment is no longer confined to the medicine show and tent show circuits of America's backwater regions. A music of homespun origin now bolsters a multi-million dollar industry and has catapulted Nashville, Tennessee, into the top ranks of America's musical entertainment centers. When entertainers with styles as disparate as those of Dean Martin, Bob Dylan, Joan Baez, and Ringo Starr journey to Nashville for recording sessions, and when singers such as Johnny Cash and Eddy Arnold present concerts before the president of the United States, one has all the evidence one needs that "the hillbilly" has passed from the American scene and that country music is no longer the neglected stepchild of our entertainment industry.

But to the country music student who has a reverence for tradition, the statistics detailing the music's commercial success can be depressing or at best ambiguous. He is pleased to see the country musicians receiving their long-overdue acclaim, but he worries about the loss of authenticity and simplicity and wonders if the music's identity will remain unblurred as its audience expands. The tradi-

101

tion-minded partisan, therefore, hopefully searches for any evidence that the music's folk roots have not been obliterated by the flood of commercialization. He sees in the proliferation of old fiddlers' contests, gospel singing conventions, and bluegrass festivals healthy cultural manifestations of an urge to return to the roots of country music, and a reminder that Nashville is not synonymous with the music. The traditionalist, while recognizing and applauding the contributions of "Music City, U. S. A.," would remind one that the music belongs to the people, and that it arose from a thousand different sources both in this country and abroad. The music is an industry, but it is also a folk art.

Country music is a direct extension of the folk music of rural white America, with its most dynamic strain deriving from the South. Beyond that, it traces its ancestry to the varied musical strains of Great Britain and Northern Europe. Its development, however, has been basically that of a cluster of North European styles successively modified, reshaped, and absorbed by a multitude of other influences. A music that has been our most "pure white" and "Anglo-Saxon," and probably our most conservative, has drawn its nourishment from many sources. What would country music be without the mandolin from Italy, the guitar from Spanish or Moorish sources, the banjo from Africa, the fiddle from India, the steel guitar from Hawaii, the string bass from Negro jazz; the yodel from Switzerland, and styles and songs from the church, the juke joint, the vaudeville stage, and Tin Pan Alley?

Rural America has never been totally isolated from the outside world; therefore, rural music has never existed in a vacuum. Even the conservative South had occasional contacts with urban America; the railroad was the symbol, but certainly not the first example, of the encroachments of industrialism. When the rural entertainer heard a new song, style, or instrument, he accepted it if it suited his sense of aesthetics, or fit in well with his community's values. And perhaps most important of all, the music was molded and preserved by the social conservatism of the South. A song or style that became too old-fashioned for the tastes of a more mobile society endured in the rural South. And as far as anyone else could tell, the song or style was country and always had been country. How many people know that such "country standards" as "Listen to the Mocking Bird," "Molly Darling," "Maple on the Hill," "Little Rosewood Casket," and "I'll Be All Smiles Tonight" came from the pens of professional composers who wrote for late-nineteenth century urban tastes?

The preceding remarks suggest then that our rural folk music was from its very beginnings partially shaped by commercial influences. Yet to many students of folk culture the word "commercial" is anathema; to such people the words "commercial" and "folk" are completely antithetical. But such a position presupposes something that never existed, a totally pure and isolated folk culture. It also falsely assumes that in our society the "folk" have rejected materialistic values and the cash nexus. Commercialism, in the long run, has done much to subvert the old folk values, but it should not be forgotten that most of us would never have been introduced to the richness and diversity of our traditional music had it not been for the performances made on radio, recordings, and personal appearances. How many folk informants faithfully passed on to folklorists versions of "Barbara Allen" which they had learned from Bradley Kincaid or Vernon Dalhart recordings?

The folk singer did not cease to be "folk" merely because he stepped in front of a microphone; the ancient oral-aural process was given a much wider scope in which to work. The audience expanded, but the orientation and social conditioning of the entertainer kept his performances geared to traditional patterns. The technological-communications revolution of the 1920's which would ultimately do so much to pull the South into the mainstream of American life also presented its rural music to the larger public for the first time.

The birth date of the country music industry, or hillbilly, as it was then called, is generally set between the years 1920-1923, the period of the coincidental convergence of both radio and phonograph recording in the exploitation of folk talent, black and white. During those years a Texas fiddler named Eck Robertson and a Virginia singer named Henry Whitter made unsolicited visits to New York recording studios to become perhaps the first hillbilly artists found on disc recordings. Hillbilly music, then, might best be understood as the commingling of the technological North with the pre-industrial South—a union of town and country, technology and agrarianism, or the rural ethos disseminated via the city. It cannot be too strongly reiterated, however, that radio and recordings did not create country music; they merely exploited an ancient phenomenon. Country music was part of the cultural baggage brought to this country by the early settlers, and its "commercialization" began virtually as early as did the life of the nation. The pre-radio commercial history of country music deserves a more careful examination by scholars than it has yet received, but we do know that country balladeers and string bands occasionally played at house parties, church socials, village dances, country fairs, political rallies, in tent shows, on riverboats, on the vaudeville circuits, and in the hundreds of medicine shows that traversed the United States during the late nineteenth and early twentieth centuries. Radio can, in fact, be considered in many ways a more sophisticated version of the old-time medicine show. Proprietary medicine firms, such as the Crazy Waters Crystals Company of Mineral Wells, Texas, began spending enormous sums of money for radio advertising in the 1930's, and employed scores of hillbilly bands such as the Monroe Brothers, Blue Sky Boys, and Mainer's Mountaineers for ballyhoo purposes. Even today, in the allegedly sophisticated 1970's, Porter Wagoner demonstrates the tenacity of the old tradition as he hawks Black Draught and Wine of Cardui on his nationally-syndicated television show.

Just as country music was not spawned by the radio and phonograph industries, neither was it foisted on an unwilling public. It has, in fact, had to make its way against every conceivable obstacle— the contempt of the "good music" people, the condescension of the commercial fraternity, and the hostility of a middle-class public who either ignored it or deemed it to be "unrespectable," the product of hayseeds or beer joint devotees. Ignored by the music trade journals, shunted on to obscure or subsidiary record labels, and assigned radio spots at times allegedly patronized only by farmers, country music was left to develop on its own in an almost subterranean manner. A string band might broadcast at 5:45 in the morning; judge the area and dimensions of its popularity through the cards and letters it received; set up a string of personal appearances by phone; personally tack up their own placards and leaflets; perform at a country schoolhouse without benefit of sound ampli-

"Eck Robertson of Amarillo" by Ann Malone

fication before an attentive audience; and then dash back to the radio station in order to make the next morning's broadcast. Somebody liked the music, however, because it survived and prospered, even during the bleak days of the depression.

It was true that the music was commercially exploited after the 1920's, but the music was still "folk" and would continue to be long after the commercial entrepreneurs moved in upon it. The performers were shaped by the same socially conservative factors that had also created their music, and they could not be anything but folk even if they tried. Most important, perhaps, was the fact that their audience shared the same musical tastes as the performers. The country repertory during its first two decades of commercial history shows a decided preference for traditional songs and ballads, both British and American. B. F. Shelton's "Pretty Polly," Vernon Dalhart's "Boston Burglar," Samantha Bumgarner's "Fly Around My Pretty Little Miss," Buell Kazee's "Lady Gay," and Gid Tanner's "Soldier's Joy" were only a few of the recordings which illustrated the hillbilly's debt to tradition. The wide provenance of the most famous Child ballad, "Barbara Allen," probably owes as much to Bradley Kincaid's recording, circulated via Sears, Roebuck catalogues, and to his performances over WLS, as it does to the east-west migration of unnamed and unknown folk balladeers. The entrepreneurs, believing that no sane or sophisticated person could like such music (unless it were performed by a trained concert singer) made little effort to market it outside the benighted South. As long as country music's milieu remained regional and the province of conservative Southerners, the performers had little incentive or desire to modify their styles. In fact, too radical a change might mean ruin to a performer's career.

While country music developed in its own fashion and, it might be added, without the incentives and advantages enjoyed by other forms of American music, the American middle class was developing its own concept of "folk" music. This was a highly romanticized concept of almost-ethereal music produced by isolated Southern mountaineers still clinging to Elizabethan ways, or lonesome music produced by cowboys on the remote ranges of the West, or the stately spirituals produced by Negroes molded by the dramatic and somber experience of slavery. The artistic concept of "folk" music was joined in the late 30's by the social concept of the folk as the struggling masses who used the ballad as a weapon in their quest for social justice. Increasingly, the words "folksong" and "protest" came to have an intellectual association which has never disappeared from the public mind. And, incidentally, in both the artistic and social usages of "folk music," the middle class almost invariably thought the music sounded much better when performed by someone other than the folk, unless one were lucky enough to find a Leadbelly or Woody Guthrie who fit the romantic stereotypes.

And notice, too, that in the growing popularization of the term "folk" there was no room for the hillbilly. This creature who developed from the folk and who sang the old-time songs in his traditional and inherited manner was ignored and scorned by the aesthetes and the intellectuals, because he did not sound like outsiders thought the folk should, and he represented a way of life that did not jibe with their preconceptions of what a folk culture should be. In the two decades prior to World War II, the Southern ruralite began to stir and moved into cities in both the North and South. The Southern migrant who moved into Southern California, or into Chicago, Detroit, or Baltimore sought out his own kind (in self defense) and frequented those institutions which gave him social cohesion and camaraderie—the storefront churches and the hillbilly taverns. And as he moved, so did hillbilly music. The reaction to him and his music, generally, was "These can't be the folk, not these clannish, dirty, foot-stomping, rebel-yelling, catsup-eating, beer-drinking rednecks!" Social customs which might have been overlooked earlier, or even considered quaint and charming a thousand miles away, could no longer be ignored.

While the socially-backward and economically-impoverished South was expelling many of its most loyal sons and daughters, rural people were changing their occupations in a significant and accelerating fashion. Farmers, and more often their sons, were becoming truck drivers and industrial workers, and as a musical consequence, the truck driving song began to supplant the historic railroad ballad. The music, too, was moving into new locales—into the dance halls or honky-tonks and out of the parlor, the barn-dance, and the church. And as the music and its clientele moved, its instrumentation and much of its content changed. With Texas musicians such as Bob Wills, Ted Daffan, Floyd Tillman, and Ernest Tubb taking the lead, song lyrics took on a more socially realistic quality as they chronicled the changing nature of lower middle-class life in America and the South. Significantly, the electric guitar (first recorded, it is believed, by Texan Bob Dunn) had made its permanent intrusion into country music by the beginning of World War II.

The combined factors of internal migration and World War II served to break down the regional character of country music and make it a national and, in fact, international phenomenon. As they had done earlier, during the Spanish-American conflict, and during the Great War of 1917, young men from all of the nation's regions mingled with each other in the military camps of World War II and traded songs and styles. Northern city boys may have been appalled at the "strange" songs and vocal inflections which bombarded their ears in the barracks or on the juke boxes in Southern taverns and dance halls, but the music entered their consciousness and often remained. The Second World War exerted revolutionary influences on American society, and its effect on music habits was no exception. While servicemen were engaging in their own form of cultural exchange, civilian industrial laborers were doing their part to broaden national music tastes. As job opportunities widened and wages increased during the heightened national defense effort, Southern rural people were, in effect, liberated from the soil and they poured by the thousands into cities all over the nation. And when they moved, they took their musical habits with them. The commercial fraternity was not long in recognizing the new developments. Adding to the work done earlier by 50,000 watt radio stations such as WLS and WSM, and the Mexican border stations, as well as by Gene Autry movies, the commercial world was ready to give country music the type of high-powered promotion that it had earlier lacked. By 1946, with performers like Eddy Arnold and Hank Williams just on the threshold of future stardom, country music was ready for its boom period; and in the twenty-five years since that time it has forced the world to take notice of it and has ceased to function as the underground of American music.

Is the music now only an indistinguishable facet of the pop music world? The music did not die when it moved to the cities; it merely

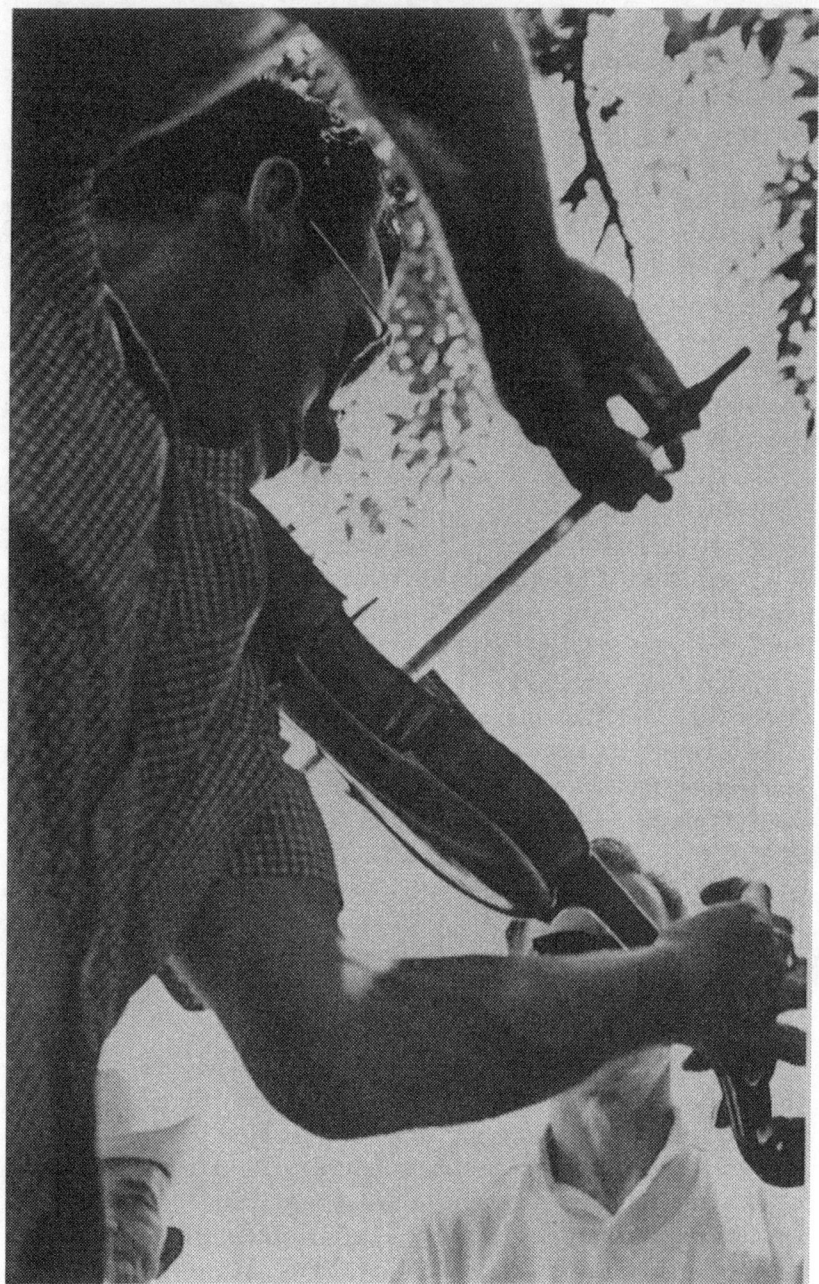

transformed its themes in order to accommodate or adapt to the new environment. The country person did not cease to be "country" just because he changed his residence or occupation. One may refer to the music as an "industry" and may prefer the word "country" to the supposedly unrespectable "hillbilly," but beneath their middle-class and business exteriors, the entertainers, for the most part, remain close to the soil. The music evolved from a rural folk heritage, and its practitioners and its most devoted followers cannot escape that heritage. Folk values cannot and will not die overnight, and their influences will still be detected for generations. Industrial, urban America has not—as any observer can see—destroyed the rural-derived values of the South. For 100 years observers have been delivering obituaries for the South, but the region still tenaciously lingers, and more significantly, the rural myth also lingers.

Even at a time of computerized complexity and moon exploration, the country music world demonstrates the survival of tradition: in the persistence of rural humor as witnessed on the "Hee Haw" and Porter Wagoner shows, the stressing of gospel material by each country entertainer (a commonplace long before the Jesus Movement made its mark on the pop music field), the burgeoning popularity of bluegrass music (the dynamic string-band and vocal style created by Bill Monroe and his imitators), and in the popularity of rural-oriented superstars such as Johnny Cash, Merle Haggard, Charley Pride, Loretta Lynn, and Dolly Parton. Most observers recognize the folk origins and orientation of such bluegrass entertainers as Bill Monroe and Ralph Stanley, but the glittering trappings of the country and western field sometimes blind us to the fact that even the superstars have at least one foot firmly planted in tradition.

Though Johnny Cash's ruffled shirt and swallow-tailed coat may suggest the image of a plantation magnate, the man emerged from and remains respectful of the small cotton farm tradition. He was born in Kingsland, Arkansas, but moved with his family to Dyess in the same state, as part of the Roosevelt Resettlement program for submarginal farmers. His songs demonstrate his loyalty to that tradition, while his marriage to June Carter, of the famous singing Carter Family, represents the symbolic union of the modern coun-

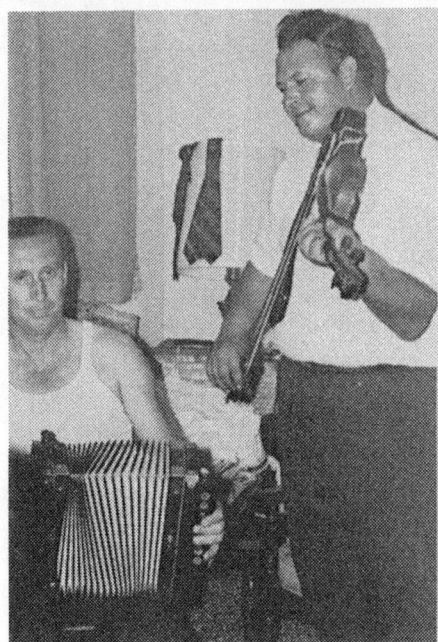

try and western singer with the older rural tradition. His occasion-ally-contrived role as a "folk-singer" a la Bob Dylan indicates the confusions concerning the word "folk." Cash does not need to go outside of his own Southern tradition to gather material for folk expression; his preoccupation with the hardcase, the drifter, and the convict (as in "Folsom Prison Blues") represents a traditional strain in country music long ago embodied in such men as Jimmie Tarlton and Jimmie Rodgers.

Merle Haggard, the youngest son of an Okie fiddler who settled in Bakersfield, California, in the 1930's, is representative of the first generation born in that state after the Okie migrations, children who were industrial in habitat but rural in orientation. While on his way to becoming one of the two or three most important coun-try singers of the 1970's, Haggard was influenced by the recordings of the honky-tonk singer Lefty Frizzell, the Texas fiddler Bob Wills, and the "father of country music," Jimmie Rodgers. Like Johnny Cash, Haggard is preoccupied with the tough guy, drifter, and common laborer (e.g., "The Fugitive," "Branded Man," "Working Man's Blues," and "Hungry Eyes") and, unlike Cash, when he sings of the convict, he speaks from experience, having served time in reform school and San Quentin Prison. When Haggard sings "Okie from Muskogee," extolling the virtues of small-town America, he probably more closely typifies the values and preju-dices of America's working class than does Pete Seeger or Joan Baez.

Women entertainers, though common in country music, did not achieve "star status" until well after World War II when Kitty Wells began competing successfully with the male performers. This factor in itself probably reflects Southern rural influence (though Women Liberationists would no doubt consider it to be illustrative of American society as a whole), because the woman was expected to remain in the home. Today, a full retinue of female entertainers dot the country music landscape, and singers like Tammy Wynette, Lynne Anderson, Loretta Lynn, and Dolly Parton approach the top male performers in record sales and audience response. In the Country Music Association's awards for 1971 Loretta Lynn was one of five nominees for "Entertainer of the Year," the only woman to receive this honor. Her own composition, "Coal Miner's Daugh-

ter," was nominated for "Song of the Year," a fitting tribute to
both her talent and her origins. The song was purely autobiographical in nature and told the story of an east Kentucky girl from
Butcher's Hollow who still remembered the sacrifices of her coal-
mining father and the hard-working mother who held the family
together. Miss Lynn, married at fifteen and a grandmother in her
early thirties, has an attractive, thoroughly country appearance, the
face and demeanor of a friendly, open, down-to-earth woman who
would look perfectly at home in a starched gingham apron making
biscuits for her family.

Dolly Parton, on the other hand, has the look of a movie starlet
or high school majorette. But don't be misled by the platinum-
blonde hair and candy-box appearance; her rural roots are authentic
and her songs are perhaps the most tradition-based in the industry
today. Although she was elected along with Porter Wagoner as the
vocal duo of the year, her song-writing talents are equally impressive. Two of her songs representative of her autobiographical
approach and respect for her mountain past are "In the Good Old
Days When Times Were Bad" and "Coat of Many Colors." In both
she realistically details both the positive and negative aspects of
rural poverty. In the first song she chronicles the harshness of the
life experienced by a farm family of fourteen in an unproductive
area of east Tennessee. In the second, she recalls the courage and in-
genuity used by her mother in the rearing of a large family in very
straited circumstances. In the song, the mother makes a coat of
patches appear beautiful rather than degrading to her child by
lovingly relating the Biblical story of Joseph's coat of many colors.

Whether the acceptance is token or genuine, both women and
black performers are within the mainstream of country music today. Ray Charles's two-volume "Modern Sounds in Country and
Western Music" did much to weaken the barriers which separated
pop and country music, and suggested also that the lines dividing
black and white music were less rigid than formerly presumed.
Some blacks evidently do listen to the Grand Ole Opry, and some
of them perform a style of music once believed to be the exclusive
province of the Southern white man. One such performer who not
only sings the "white man's music" but does it more competently
than most whites is the Country Music Association's "Entertainer

of the Year," Charley Pride. Even if he were not a top-flight entertainer, Pride would still be a phenomenon. He is the Jackie
Robinson of country music, the first black country singer to be
recorded on a major label (RCA Victor). As a black singer Charley
Pride reminds us of the old and continuing contributions made by
black musicians, mostly unknown and unsung, to the country
music field.

Though he may be atypical in many important respects, Pride's
origins parallel those of many white country performers. He was
born into a cotton sharecropper's family in Sledge, Mississippi, and
apparently shares many of the assumptions and values held by his
white colleagues. Many explanations might be given for his success,
but the most convincing is the fact that he is both good and
country; he possesses a style, in fact, that is more rural than most
of the people who profess to be country entertainers. In short,
Charley Pride is more traditional than most. He shuns the gaudy
garb favored by many of the stars, and with a dignified Bill Monroe-
like bearing, sings songs dealing with universal themes in a straight-
forward, no-nonsense, tightly controlled delivery. If country music
remains distinctive and close to its traditional roots, it may some
day be recorded that a black man, Charley Pride, helped to turn
the music around while demonstrating that the hard-country sounds
could also be commercial.

Why has the music survived and prospered?

Country music can be viewed not only as a perpetuation of folk
and rural patterns but as an expression of the enduring South.
Viewed in this light, therefore, country music might be interpreted
as a form of cultural nationalism. Experiencing its commercial
birth in the 1920's when the South was under siege as a reactionary
region (and when has the South not been under siege?), the music
still survives and thrives today. By preserving the music and trans-
planting it in those areas to which he has migrated, the rural
Southerner still demonstrates unassimilability. The music exerts
the same function that folk music has always played—it plays a
conservative role in providing social cohesion and identification for
a people uprooted from their traditional culture. Country music
can partially be understood as a music of alienation, a dirge com-
memorating the old departed home, and a rallying cry, or rebel

yell if you will, to call together like-minded souls in a new environment—the music of a people who see the world changing around them with bewildering speed, and a world in which all of the old, well-ordered values and assumptions seem to be disintegrating. Country music lyrics express the confusion of values and the shattering of social ties, as witnessed by the profusion of songs dealing with the problems of drink, marital infidelity, the breakup of homes, and the decline of faith. But on the other hand, the songs also demonstrate a desire for the perpetuation of those values believed to be basically "American": traditional Christianity (with a fundamentalist tinge), family and home solidarity, patriotism of an almost jingoistic variety, nativism, conventional morality, and ordered and traditional race relationships.

It should not be surprising, then, to hear of the admiration for George Wallace felt by many country entertainers. They and George come out of the same culture, and they share the same ideals. In 1968 Music Row in Nashville was considered to be virtually a command post for George Wallace. At the same time, it should not surprise anyone to hear of the mutual love affair between country music and the Silent Majority. (Harlan Howard's most recent album is dedicated "to the silent majority, with love.") Both are affluent, both are tradition-oriented, and both are uncertain of their status. The country entertainer is torn, as always, between two worlds— the world of folk simplicity from which he came, and the world of middle-class respectability for which he yearns.

Wherever the rural Southerner goes, to Detroit, to Cincinnati, to California, or anywhere in the world, when he takes his music with him, he also takes a little bit of home. For millions of transplanted Southerners, country music is the music of home—because it is more than just an isolated musical expression, it is bound up with the security patterns and values that helped to make him the person he is. And, correspondingly, detractors have not always understood that in attacking the music they attack more than the music. Northern and city boys perhaps did not understand during World War II that when they ridiculed Roy Acuff in the barracks and on troop ships they also ridiculed the culture from which Acuff and his fans came. And if one attacked the culture, he also attacked Mother, the country church, the old home, the South.

Country music takes the Southerner back home whether he be a reluctant emigree like the Okie or Appalachian mountaineer, or a willing exile like the liberal, and today, with our nation becoming over-organized and urbanized, perhaps the music takes many people, many of whom never lived in the South or in the country, back to a way of life that existed, or presumably existed, before mass society made its inroads in the United States.

HORSE PENNING: SOUTHEAST TEXAS, 1913

Bill Brett

I'VE read many stories about cowboys and cowmen, but I haven't found much about the "hands" in my part of the country, southeast Texas. This is the part that lays between the Sabine and the Trinity at the south edge of the Big Thicket.

Southeast Texas was one of the last free-range areas in Texas. Fifteen years ago the town man finally mustered enough votes to pass a stock law. He did get the stock off the highway and streets and was able to take down his yard fence, but for many East Texans the stock law was a mixed blessing. Why? Fences and more fences. Not hundreds but thousands of acres that had always been open to the public to hunt and fish on were fenced in and posted. The big lumber companies leased their lands to cattlemen and hunting clubs, who fenced it and posted it and left the lone hunter out. Now only the razorback hog comes and goes as he will. That cranky, independent animal has never recognized either the stock law or a man's right to say, "This is my land and you'll not use it." More power to the hogs, I say.

All of this leads up to a yarn I heard years ago. I'll see if I can quit rambling and get back on the track. I heard this from a fellow who was part cowhand, part farmer, part sawmill worker, and all man. He told it something like this:

"One time me and my brother Tom was heading home from the

117

shipping pens at Walter and got into the damndest horse race I've ever been in. We'd been working for Mr. Partlow gathering and shipping beeves for a couple of weeks and had got through the night before. We'd been paid off and laid off that morning and had caught our private horses and was headed home. We was young fellows, about seventeen or eighteen, but we was good hands and Mr. Partlow was a good man to work for, paid a whole dollar a day and didn't crowd you, give you fifteen or sixteen hours a day to earn it in. We had $14 apiece and was rich country boys.

"We'd crossed Long Island Creek and had just rode out into that big cone that lays between it and Walker Marsh when we seen a bunch of broomtail ponies about the middle of it. There was lots of horses in this country then and plenty of range for them, and they was something we was always interested in so we was looking these over pretty close and them us.

"Directly they started to trot off and we seen a saddled horse in the bunch. We knowed right off what we'd found. Frank Dowdell was breaking a horse for one of the Jordans, and about three weeks before he'd piled Frank over his head. During his trip from saddle to ground, Frank's belt buckle had hung the top of the headstall and he'd took the bridle with him. The bunch the horse took up with mostly ranged Long Island woods so it was understandable why he hadn't been seen. Frank was offering $10.00 to whoever penned the horse and that was ten days pay.

"A man didn't have much chance running horses in the woods without dogs, but Tom and me figured since we was on fresh horses we'd try it. There was only about a quarter mile of woods between the cone and Batiste Prairie, and if we could get them through there we'd have a chance. They must of just watered. When we hit the woods we was siding them and not giving them no chance to turn either way. I could hear Tom whooping and knew he was holding his place but I was too busy fightin' brush to answer much. A limb almost took me out of the saddle and I lost most of my shirt, but me and Tom both come out close enough to the horses to keep them from crossing in front of us and going back in the woods.

"With them on the prairie it was easier. Just hard riding and watching for holes. Running cattle a horse generally watches for things but running horses he's watching them as close as you are. Anyway, in a couple of hours we had them going pretty good and could half-way drive them. One old mare couldn't stand to be crowded but otherwise they was doing good.

"Old man Phipps was living on the lower end of Batiste then, and we was trying to get them to his place to pen them. We finally crowded them against his field fence and was dividing that $10.00 when that old fool mare seen them pens coming up and hell broke loose. She left with the bunch following, and me and Tom went to riding to get there.

"I was on a little bay pony that had lots of bottom but was too slow to head them but Tom was a-horseback. He had a big one-eyed sorrel, a West Texas horse that one of the Dew boys had brought into this country, and that big devil could run. I was plumb out of the race by the time Tom headed and turned them back.

"We was both whooping every jump, thinking we'd get some help from the Phipps. I could see a saddled horse tied to the front fence and about the time we got the horses back against the field fence I seen a man on the way to him and could see a woman in the back yard turning some dogs loose. I hollered to Tom to stay with them, help was coming. We'd stopped the horses against the fence but that old wild mare was still wanting to go. Anyway, I had time to watch toward the house and the next thing that happened was something to see.

"The Phipps hadn't been in that country long but we'd already heard that the old man was a little absent-minded and this he demonstrated. He straddled that old horse and hung the spurs to him. He'd of had a good running start after that if he'd of untied the bridle reins from the fence. The first jump he made jerked a panel of pickets down and the second jump jerked the panel under him. There weren't no third jump. Man and horse was both down and the pickets was flying.

"I seen a couple of women heading for him but the horses, led by the old mare, started again and I didn't have time to watch any more. They'd no more than started, though, when help arrived. The two dogs, both yellow black-mouthed curs that the women had turned loose, got there. One of them was a real smart aleck. That old mare was doing her best to get around Tom when that ole puppy fastened her in the nose and stood her on her head. That about done it. One more time she tried but when them teeth popped in front of her nose she give up. The Phipps girls had the pen gates fixed right by then and, with the dogs working ahead, it was no trouble to drive the bunch in.

"We closed the gate and went to the house to get water and see about the old man. He was up patching the fence and him, Mrs. Phipps, and the five girls was all laughing about what happened.

"The Phipps had some mighty pretty girls. The five ranged from fourteen to twenty-one and had half the young bucks in the country hanging around. Tom and me had seen the family a time or two but wasn't really acquainted until that day Tom got so acquainted that in the next six months he nearly starved a horse to death tied to the old man's fence courting the middle girl.

"Well, we cooled and visited awhile and then went back to the pen. I roped the saddled horse and worked him into another pen, him acting like a wild'un all the way. He quieted down after me and Tom caught him and got a hitch on his nose. He was girth-rubbed bad and pretty well ganted but in good shape otherwise. Tom made a bosal with his rope and put it on him and we was ready to go but nothing would do the Phipps but we had to stay and eat dinner. They was awful good people, laughed and joked a lot. All gone now. The old man and Mrs. Phipps died with the flu in 1918 and the girls married and moved off.

"We finally got off about the middle of the evening, Tom leading the horse and me carrying the saddle. Got to Frank's a little before dark. He was glad to get his saddle back but didn't seem too proud to see that ole bronc. Told me later he didn't have any more trouble breaking him out but he never was fit for nothing. No bottom and handled hisself like a cow. He paid me and Tom with the last $10.00 gold piece I ever seen. We made it in home around eleven that night and was glad to get there. That $38.00 didn't do me and Tom much good though. Pa used most of it paying taxes and buying seed the next spring."

SAN JACINTO, AS SHE WAS: OR, WHAT REALLY HAPPENED ON THE PLAIN OF ST. HYACINTH ON A HOT APRIL AFTERNOON IN 1836

R. Henderson Shuffler

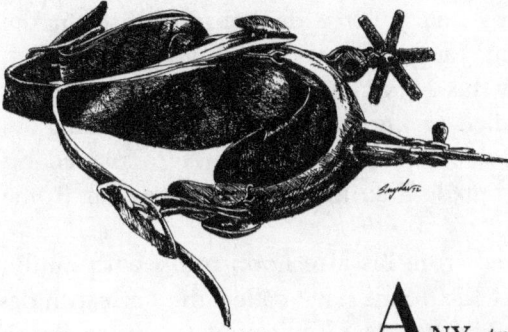

ANY true Texan can, and with only slight provocation, will, hold forth gustily for hours on the glories of the Battle of San Jacinto. With a few drinks under his belt, he is apt to sing a chorus or two of "The Yellow Rose of Texas," as his patriotic fervor mounts. But, he isn't likely ever to tell you about Emily Morgan. He probably never heard of her.

Yet, Emily, a comely quadroon servant girl from the Texas plantation of Col. James Morgan, was the real heroine, after a peculiar fashion, of the battle in which Texas won its independence. And there is some indication that she was the original "Yellow Rose," immortalized somewhat anonymously in that oft-heard Texas song.

The story has been told many times of how, on the afternoon of April 21, 1836, a band of ragged Texans, 783 in number, crawled through the high grass of the San Jacinto Plain to sneak up on the camp where some 1,360 Mexican soldiers lolled in the shade of the post oak trees which crowned a slight rise. At a quarter past 4 o'clock, the Texans came within firing range of their unsuspecting enemies and rose, with blood-curdling shouts, to charge the hostile camp to the unlikely tune of a lilting old English love ballad.

This much of their history is familiar to most Texans, as well as the outcome, with 630 Mexicans dead, 208 wounded, the balance prisoners, and Texas free. Less familiar, and certainly never included in the pompous orations of our professional patriots, is the story of Emily Morgan. Yet there is genuine reason to doubt that the handful of undisciplined Texans would have swept over the veteran Mexican troops in eighteen blood-curdling minutes, without her assistance.

Emily was the M'latta Houri, in a manner of speaking, of the Texas Revolution. She, it was, who turned President-General Antonio López de Santa Anna y Pérez de Lebrón loose on the bloody battlefield of San Jacinto in his red slippers and silken drawers, too late to rally his Mexican legions to face the Texan onslaught and too befuddled to know for sure what was going on. She had played the Napoleon of the West like Nero played his fiddle, and whilst they had made their music, a lot more than Rome had burned.

Before he fully recovered from his afternoon romp with Emily, Santa Anna had lost what historians have called the sixteenth decisive battle of history, and with it, Mexican claims to a huge chunk of North America. It can be accurately said that Emily swapped her questionable virtue for approximately a million square miles of the American West, which comes close to an all-time high in the market for the most ancient of commercial products. In the bargain, she turned the trick in the middle of the afternoon, in a silken tent pitched in the midst of an army encamped for battle.

It is a sad commentary on human nature that the memory of Emily Morgan is almost lost in the limbo of time. No one knows whether she survived the carnage on the plain of Saint Hyacinth, or not. No trace of her can be found, after that day.

But, a careful perusal of old Texas histories, personal papers and documents, definitely establishes her reality. Although she was literally an undercover agent, going into action in no other uniform than her satin-smooth beige birthday suit, Emily played a vital role in the winning of Texas' liberty. Her contribution to the sudden and surprising victory of a raggle-taggle handful of Texans over a trained and well-armed Mexican army twice their number was at least as important as those of General Sam Houston, Col. Mirabeau Lamar, or any of the other dashing heroes Texans brag so much about today.

Col. James Morgan, promoter and leading businessman of the town of New Washington, located on Morgan's Point, a few miles below the plain of San Jacinto, told Emily's story to William Bollaert, a famous British visitor to Texas, in 1838. Bollaert included it in his memoirs. Col Morgan was in a position to know the facts, Emily had been one of this slaves.

Major George Erath, well-educated and thoroughly reliable gentleman of Austrian birth, who fought on the Texan side, later reported that "our victory was made much easier by Santa Anna's voluptuousness." Several Mexican historians have referred to "Santa Anna's quadroon mistress during the Texas campaign." It seems high time that Emily's story was brought out of the footnotes and veiled allusions of history into the open.

The full story, as it emerges, in bits and pieces, from the scattered records, is worth preserving.

Emily was a winsome, light-skinned product of the bedroom integration so popular in the South of that period. She was born a slave and at an early age became the property of James Morgan, prosperous and enterprising North Carolina merchant. In 1831, when Morgan decided to move his base of business operations to the new and fertile fields of the Mexican province of Texas, he was faced with a serious problem. The Mexican government had forbidden the importation of slaves into its territory and much of his capital was tied up in slaves. Morgan solved the problem by the simple expedient of "freeing" his sixteen slaves in one breath and indenturing them as servants for 99 years, in the next.

Thus, in mid-April of 1836, when Emily approached her moment of glory, she was nominally free, nearly white and approximately twenty-one. According to contemporary reports she was also bouncy, beguiling and built like nobody's business. She was a fitting candidate for lyric perpetuation as "The Yellow Rose of Texas."

In case you didn't know, the original published version of that recently desegregated lyric, printed in New York just before the Civil War, sang of "the sweetest Rose of color this darkey ever knew." It was published for use in Negro minstrel shows and the reference to a yellow "Rose of color" was plainly understood at the time as meaning a mulatto girl. Our Emily may well have been the original Yellow Rose. Her story, widely known and often retold in Texas in the 1840's, was the stuff of which folk songs were customarily made. The Tin Pan Alleys of those days were no more given to originality than those of today, and most of the minstrel tunes were merely steals from the folk songs of the period. One recently published Texas history mentions old lyrics of "The Yellow Rose of Texas" which sing of "Emily, the Maid of Morgan's Point."

In the spring of 1836, Emily was unquestionably the belle of the boardwalks in the sleepy little shipping town of New Washington, located at the tip of Morgan's Point, a slight peninsular projection of Southeast Texas, jutting out into the Bay of San Jacinto. Her deliberately provocative amble down the street on a hot afternoon was probably the most exciting event in town, for the male population, at least. The war was a long way off.

Word of the fall of the Alamo, in early March, had stirred folks up for a while, but the disheartening news of repeated Texas retreats before the advancing Mexican armies had let them down again. Some said old Sam Houston didn't seem to want to fight. He just chewed a lot of tobacco and cussed loud, drank whiskey and courted that widow Mann. Every time the Mexicans came close, he pulled up stakes and retreated again.

For the past two or three weeks he had been holed up in the Brazos bottoms near the Groce plantation, while the Mexicans moved up on all sides. There were even reports that one Mexican army had crossed the Brazos and was on the way to the capitol at Harrisburg. This report was confirmed on April 16th, when the big shots of the Texas government started streaming into New Washington, in a hurry to catch a boat over to Galveston Island.

Late that same day the excitement picked up, as a troop of Mexican cavalry showed up on the heels of the flying Texans. There were stories around town that Texas' President Burnet and his wife, last of the government family to reach the docks, had barely cleared land in a skiff, on their way out to the steamer, when the Mexicans dashed up. Some of the soldiers raised their muskets. but an officer stopped them, because he saw a woman in the skiff.

Colonel Almonte, who commanded the Mexican cavalrymen, did his best to keep them under control, but after they broke into the big Morgan warehouse and found whiskey, along with other supplies, they went on the loose. That night and the next day were about the wildest New Washington had seen in its somewhat lurid history.

Then around noon on the 18th, the Mexican infantry arrived, dragging a good-sized cannon, and followed by a train of packmules loaded with supplies and ammunition. At the head of this army of around 1,000 troops was none other than General Santa Anna, himself. At 42, "the Napoleon of the West," as he liked to be called, enjoyed a world-wide reputation, which had reached even to such remote spots as New Washington. President of Mexico, General of the Mexican Army and a warrior noted both for his victories and for his ruthless cruelties, he also held the undisputed title of the most notorious wencher in all Mexico. (This was the practical equivalent of a world championship.)

Now at the height of his career and vigor, Santa Anna was doing his best to live up to all phases of his reputation. Wherever he might be, he indulged his legendary appetites for gambling and women. He drank with some restraint, but made up for this by free and frequent use of opium. Since the long marches across barren deserts and short but painful struggles through the Texas riverbottom mud had made it impractical for him to bring his usual retinue of entertainers on this campaign, he was now foraging off the country, taking the good things of life where he found them.

At San Antonio, late in February, he had found what looked like a good thing, a luscious 17-year-old beauty named Melchora Iniega Barrera. Unfortunately, she was a bit prim, refusing to play without benefit of clergy. He had moved into the Barrera home, turned on his famous charm, lavished gifts and, finally, threats, on Melchora and her widowed mother. At last, in desperation, he had arranged for one of his sergeants, an Irishman who had once been an actor, to disguise himself as a priest and perform a fake marriage. Thus he attained the desired Barrera end.

While the siege of the Alamo was under way, the Napoleon of the West spent most of his time honeymooning with his new "bride," letting his generals fight the badly outnumbered, but stubborn Texans. Even after the Alamo fell, Santa Anna dallied in old San Antonio, while his armies ranged over Texas, seeking what he believed to be the last remnants of the rebel forces. When, on March 31, he finally was persuaded by his generals that the war was not really over and could use his personal attention, he set out to follow his armies in style.

In a luxurious coach drawn by six white mules and escorted by half a hundred gaudily uniformed dragoons, Santa Anna and Melchora rode out of San Antonio, followed by an imposing train of aides, luggage and supplies. Three days later, the going was becoming rough and the resplendent entourage of the conqueror was becoming bedraggled. At the swollen Guadalupe River, Santa Anna finally saw that travel in style would be impossible. He called one of his trusted aides and sent him back to Mexico with the coach, carrying the beauteous Melchora and a chest of silver coin he had filched from his campaign funds. That was on April 3.

Santa Anna was obviously a man who got lonesome in a hurry. When he rode into New Washington, on April 18, 1836, he had been sharing his silken campaign tent with nothing more interesting than his prize game cock for two full weeks. His roving eye soon lit on the lithesome figure of our Emily, somewhere on the sidelines, watching the excitement. In no time, Emily was commandeered to fill a niche in the Santa Anna entourage. Her niche became a very important fixture in the Santa Anna household.

It is quite likely that Emily was both flattered and intrigued by her sudden rise to recumbent eminence. Santa Anna was considered quite a connoisseur of women. He had started young and worked assiduously at his favorite indoor sport. With a roving eye, more than an ordinary share of good looks and dash and a reputation for being quite generous with his mistresses, he was not unattractive to a gal on the make.

The lurid details of just what Emily did for, to, or with, the Mexican dictator are not available. The results, however, speak for themselves. After less than two days and nights with Emily, the General was apparently completely unmanned.

Colonel Pedro Delgado, Santa Anna's military aide in the Texas campaign, later reported that on the morning of April 20, the Mexican Army had completed sacking New Washington and was ready to move on. "At about eight o'clock A.M.," Delgado wrote, "everything was ready for the march . . . when Captain Barragan rushed in at full speed, reporting that Houston was close on our rear.

"There is in front of New Washington a dense wood, through which runs a narrow lane about half a league in length, allowing passage to packmules in single file only, and to mounted men in double file. This land was filled with our pickets, the drove of mules, and the remainder of the detachment. His excellency and staff were still in town. Upon hearing Barragan's report, he leaped on his horse and galloped off at full speed for the lane, which being crowded with men and mules, did not afford him as prompt an exit as he wished. However, knocking down one and riding over another, he overcame the obstacles, shouting at the top of his voice: 'THE ENEMY ARE COMING! THE ENEMY ARE COMING!' "

The junior officers finally managed to calm their men and catch their mules and commander. In an hour or so the Mexican army was on the march, up the coast to the open prairie where history was to be made. By two in the afternoon, when they reached the plain of San Jacinto, the general, with the help of a few sniffs of his private store of opium, had regained his courage.

He made a pass at the Texans, who were camped in a sheltering wood on the far side of the plain, but, unable to draw them out, drew back to a wood along the river and encamped. Time was in his favor, he believed. His brother-in-law, General Cós, was on the way with some 400 reinforcements, and he could afford to wait until these swelled his army to well over twice the number of the Texans.

On the morning of the 21st, Santa Anna was up early, apparently fresh as a daisy and full of confidence (or opium). His able officers, including the gallant General Castrillón, tried to point out to him that his camp was not the most advantageous spot to defend, but he brushed them off and returned to his tent, and Emily.

Delgado reports that he mentioned the matter to General Castrillón, and the latter swore roundly, commenting: "I know it well, but I cannot help it. You know that nothing prevails here against the caprice, arbitrary will, and ignorance of that man!"

This conversation, Delgado says, took place just outside Santa Anna's silken tent, in a tone sufficiently loud to be easily heard inside, but the commander was either not listening, or had his mind on other matters. When Cós and his men arrived, around nine in the morning, Santa Anna told them to unsaddle their horses, fall out and eat and rest. Then, apparently, he went back to his love-making.

Around four-thirty in the afternoon, all was quiet in the Mexican camp. The tired soldiers, after a heavy meal, were lounging in the edge of the woods, napping or swapping lies. Santa Anna was in his tent, as he later claimed, taking a siesta. The indications are he slightly misspelled the word. He should have said "fiesta."

Suddenly, all Hell broke loose. The Texans had slipped out of their woods and silently stolen across the plain until they were in easy shooting distance of the unsuspecting foe. Then old Sam Houston, riding in front of them on a fine white stallion, raised his sword high above his head and bellowed: "Fire away! God damn you, fire!"

A raucous little band made up of three fifes in the hands of infantrymen and a drum beat by a big Negro named Dick from New Orleans, struck up a bawdy ballad, "Will You Come to the Bower?" Whether the Texans had figured out just how Santa Anna was occupied at the moment, or not, we do not know, but the lyrics of the tune they chose for one of the bloodiest charges in history ran:

> Will you come to the bower I have shaded for you?
> Our bed shall be roses all spangled with dew.
> Will you come to the bower I have shaded for you?
> Our bed shall be roses all spangled with dew.
> Will you, will you, will you, will you come to the bower?
> Will you, will you, will you, will you come to the bower?
>
> There under the bower of roses you'll lie
> With a blush on your cheek, but a smile in your eye. . .etc.

The minute the Texans opened fire at close range with their assorted rifles, pistols and shotguns, accompanied by a withering hail of old nails, chains, horseshoes and assorted scrap-iron from their two small cannons, the battle was practically over. They accompanied this terrible fire with wild shouts of "Remember the Alamo!" and "Remember Goliad!" striking terror into the hearts of Mexicans who had participated in those massacres.

At this moment, Delgado reports, "I saw his excellency running about in the most excited manner, wringing his hands and unable to give an order."

Santa Anna had dashed out of his tent, clad only in a fine linen shirt and his silken drawers. Seeing the slaughter of his forces, he grabbed the nearest horse, a fine stallion named "Old Whip," which one of his officers had commandeered the day before from a near-by ranch, and lit out for the tall timber. What Emily started, in the way of taking Santa Anna for a ride, Old Whip finished. The head-strong horse, instead of carrying him to safety and a possible contact with his sizable armies on the Brazos, headed for the home ranch on the edge of the battlefield. There Santa Anna found some old clothes in an abandoned shack. These he donned to ward off the cold of the approaching night, and in these he was captured the next afternoon.

It was too bad that "the Napoleon of the West," who prided himself on his knowledge of military history, had not made a closer study of the American Revolution. Otherwise, during that chilly and desperate night of hiding in the bottoms of Vince's Bayou, he could have consoled himself with the similar fate of a certain Major General Richard Prescott, commander of the British forces in Rhode Island, under Lord Howe.

One winter evening General Prescott left his headquarters to spend the night at the house of one Mr. Overing, near Newport, where the bedwarmers were reported to have most interesting shapes and entertaining agility.

Around midnight a troop of American soldiers surrounded the house and captured the general, in bed, without clothing. This led the staid *London Press* to print, in connection with the story of "General Prescott being carried off naked, unannointed, unanneal-ed," the following quatrain:

> What various lures there are to ruin man;
> Woman, the first and foremost, all bewitches!
> A nymph thus spoiled a general's mighty plan
> And gave him to the foe—without his breeches!

And what of Emily? No historian seems to know. None, certainly, has recorded her fate after the battle of San Jacinto.

At least one woman among the Mexican camp-followers was re-ported to have been killed by the Texans in the excitement and confusion of the wholesale slaughter which followed their charge. A number of others were captured. But, regardless of her mortal fate, the fame of Emily was a living thing in Texas and certain circles in Mexico, for years to come. The story haunted Santa Anna, but did not seriously impede his careers of debauchery and political intrigue. He lived to become the Mexican head of state, either as president or dictator, four more times in his long and lurid life.

But, he never regained Texas. It became a proud republic, then a state of the North American union, and finally a practically ecstatic state of mind. Yet, in all this time, with all its wealth, Texas has never, so far, made even a token acknowledgment of its debt to the Yellow Rose of long ago, whose end played such an important role in its beginning.

A hardy band of Texas history buffs is quietly forming now, pledged to the eventual correction of this inequity. Under the title of "The Knights of the Yellow Rose," they have assumed the portentous task of leading Old Man Texas up to the lick log.

Some moonlit April night they plan to meet beside the towering monument which marks the battlefield of San Jacinto (several feet higher than the Washington monument, as any Texan will readily remind you). There they will plant a small patch of pussywillow, encircling a garden of yellow roses. And in the center, a modest stone, on which will be engraved this legend:

In Honor of Emily
Who Gave Her All for Texas
Piece by Piece

SINGING ALL DAY & DINNER ON THE GROUNDS

Francis Edward Abernethy

BY the time we got to Harris Chapel the singing had already started. The Sacred Harp singers of this part of East Texas, near Marshall, had gathered for their one hundredth annual all-day singing and dinner on the grounds. The meeting house was large, white, many-windowed and frame, and it sat in a clearing near the community cemetery where old cedars stood. The parking area was shaded by post oaks, and surrounding all were the pines. Sam Asbury pretty well described the sound of a full house of Old Harp singers when he recalled, "The immediate din was tremendous; at a hundred yards it was beautiful; at a distance of a half mile it was magnificent." We parked somewhere in the "beautiful" range and could feel the music roll over us before it flowed away into the surrounding woods.

We went in with the guilt a city man feels from violating a time schedule, but there was no need to worry. There is no body of people more casual in their comings and goings than Sacred Harpers. Children wander about among their aunts and uncles, and there is frequent rotation among the members on the singing benches. They are as comfortable and unselfconscious with their singing as they are at their own supper tables.

We got ourselves situated and there was no doubt about it; we were, according to Asbury, in the "tremendous" range and those mighty Old Harp singers were pounding out their songs to the greater glory of the Lord.

131

Sacred Harp music—named from the 1844 songbook *The Sacred Harp*—has been preserved mainly by the Primitive Baptists, although in the beginning most of the lower churches in the South sang the same music. Even now many regular Sacred Harp singers are from denominations other than Primitive Baptist. The survival of the music and the tradition, however, has been dependent upon the beliefs and attitudes of the Primitive Baptists. They are fundamentalists who have followed their selected portions of the Bible to the letter and have arrived at a belief in predestination. For that reason they don't have revivals and they don't send out missionaries, and they are easy to be with. You don't have to worry about their trying to save you or get you to join the church. They leave matters of the soul to God, and a man is either saved or he isn't. To me this is a chancy philosophy that puts man's afterlife in the position of a pig in a poke, but the results of their belief in the doctrine of the elect is impressive in them. They move with a serenity that is born of confidence in a life to come that is more than the usual mouthings of the wishful thinkers, and I guess I envy them some.

Primitive Baptists are also called Hardshell Baptists because of the uncrackable shell of their beliefs, and foot-washing Baptists because of their observance of that little practiced ritual. Foot washing sounds sort of odd when you first think about their doing it in church. And I never will forget how one fine old lady down in the Thicket would rock and chuckle about how her mother used to wash her feet with bleach, trying to get them presentable for foot washing. But it's not funny when you are there. It is very moving and impressive. They kneel and wash their brother's feet and then embrace and ask forgiveness for the sins they might have committed against each other. At Appleby one Sunday toward the end of foot washing, everybody began singing "Amazing Grace," softly and with the characteristic Sacred Harp minor chords, and there wasn't a dry eye in the church.

The Hardshells don't have paid preachers or Sunday schools and they don't take up offerings and they don't have musical instruments. But they get along well enough without these adornments. The pastor sometimes preaches at as many as six different churches during the month's circuit, and he doesn't get a salary for it; he

works at his regular job during the week. Instead of having Sunday
school, the heads of the families are supposed to teach their children about the Bible. When the church needs money the elders let
it be known how much and what for and the congregation scrapes
it up among themselves. Or, if the church needs repairing, the members show up with their hammers and nails and fix it. And the main
thing they don't have is a piano or organ or some other kind of
mechanical music box. The Lord be eternally praised that they decided that "Singing with grace in your hearts to the Lord" meant
that they were supposed to sing *acapella*. Otherwise some of the
strongest and most beautiful music in the world would have been
marred beyond measure.

The south end of the Harris Chapel meeting house was a raised
platform with a pulpit or speaker's stand, depending on what the
building was being used for at the time. The thirty or forty main
singers sat two or three deep in a hollow square just below the
platform, and the leader stood in the middle. They were divided
into four groups. The altos sat with their backs to the platform.
The basses sat to their right. Across from and facing the altos sat
the leads (the soprano line), backed up by the audience, most of
whom sang the lead with them. On the leads' right sat what they
call the "tribbles" (the tenor, or treble, line). Except for the basses,
all the singing parts were integrated, male and female. If some
female were to show up, however, who sang a pretty good bass, she
would probably be welcomed to that section.

The Harris Chapel singers were following the tradition: everybody got to lead two songs. The song leader finished his pair and
called on his successor. A man arose from the bass section and asked
whether number eighty-two had been "used" yet. It had not, so
a stout gentleman in the "tribbles" sang the note names for the four
parts: "Faw, sol, law, faw!" Everybody got his note, the leader's
hand came down, and they began their musical march through
"Bound for Canaan" as strongly as Cromwell's Puritan Roundheads
descended on Charles' Cavaliers at Marston Moor, singing only the
old Elizabethan fasola notes the first time around and then going
into the words.

Compared to Sacred Harp singing, First Church music is water to
wine. They sing with a power and a vitality and involvement that

makes the song a living work of art. The sound is strong and the beat is regular and heavy, and the leader and most of the singers pound and saw the air in time to the beat. This is singer's music, not listeners. Those in the audience who don't sing, follow the song attentively, and many of them follow the words in their books. The singers don't sing to entertain or to pass a few minutes from the hour's meeting time. They sing their pleas and prayers directly to their God.

W. B. Yeats, in his poem "Sailing to Byzantium," said that when he died he wanted to come back, to live again, as a work of art. This to him was Nirvana, the highest point that man could reach. Old Harp singers are close to becoming a work of art. They blend themselves so completely with the sound and sense of the music that the singers become the song.

When the leader has lead his two songs he calls on another. Everybody gets to lead; it's both a duty and a privilege. Old men who can hardly sing any more are helped into the square by their loving fellows who help them once again make their musical affirmation of the grace that is their personal gift from God. The strong men sing stronger for them, and the old-timers sit down feeling that they are still helping roll the world along.

As to the music, beyond the fact that the doleful and Asiatic minor chords cause the music to differ from the conventional First Church sound, the tunes have an ancient heritage and the words have a definite philosophical cast of their own.

Most of the tunes are English, Irish, Scottish, and Welsh folk melodies. They originated somewhere in the lost past and have been handed down from one generation to another for hundreds of years. The tunes have shifted and changed with the times and the singers and have carried the burden of all sorts of secular songs before some preacher used them as the vehicle for his message.

Sacred Harp had its beginning during the time of the Great Revival on the southern upland and lowland frontiers at the end of the eighteenth century. The people involved were for the most part rural and illiterate, and they were reacting against the austerity of New England Calvinism and the tunelessness of Calvinist Psalm singing. Like the Wesleys in England, the frontier ministers had large and emotional congregations of Presbyterians, Baptists, and

Methodists but no songs to sing. And they had to bolster their
faith that there would be a better world hereafter if they could
just get through the here and now. So the preachers and the versi-
fiers took the tunes that the people did know, the folk songs that
their ancestors had brought with them from the old countries,
songs like "Barbara Allen," "Lord Randall," or "The Blue-eyed
Stranger," and put holy words to the sinful songs. A Sacred Harp
song that illustrates this parodying of folk music is called "Plenary,"
or "Hark! From the Tombs." It is still used by some Masonic
groups as a funeral dirge, and is sung as a dead march to the Scottish folk tune of "Auld Lang Syne."

> Hark! from the tomb a doleful sound,
> Mine ears, attend the cry:
> "Ye living men, come view the ground
> Where you must shortly lie.
> (Chorus)
> Where you must shortly lie,
> Where you must shortly lie,
> Ye living men, come view the ground
> Where you must shortly lie.

The words to "Plenary" are not over 150 years old, but the folk
tune goes back several hundred years, and the memento mori,
remembrance-of-death theme was old in the Middle Ages.

This memento mori theme is characteristic of Sacred Harp music,
and that separates it as much as anything I can think of from modern music, church or otherwise. The only ones who keep remind-
ing us of our eventual and inevitable trip to the grave are the in-
surance salesmen. We don't concern ourselves much about the
hereafter, and we think as little as possible about the death that
every man owes life. As a result, maybe we have lost some of life's
seasoning. Eternal night or a live-long day would be as boring as
thoughts of an everlasting Paradise. What makes October so sweet
and beautifully mellow is our knowing that the year is nearing the
end of its time. And life is precious in a direct ratio to our knowledge of its ephemerality. You have got to know death if you want
to give life its due.

The words of the Old Harp songs are often sad and mournful. The verses, many of them, were written by people who knew too much of this world's suffering because they lived on land that was barely subdued. They weren't romanticizing when they wrote, "Time . . . Swift as an Indian arrow flies." The Southerners who formed the Sacred Harp tradition were those strong and violent natures that made up the first waves of all frontiers. They were emotionally forceful or they wouldn't have started out in the first place, and they couldn't have stuck in the second. As a result of the harsh land they lived in, the death that roamed swiftly among them, and their own tumultuous spirits, they lived lives that teetered on the edge of catastrophe. They felt themselves buffeted in a world where they seemed to have very little control, so their philosophy became fatalistic. "Whatever will be, will be," they said, repeating the philosophy of their Anglo-Saxon ancestors in the time of Beowulf; and because they had no control over the awful powers of nature and life, they handed the responsibility over to their God. They decided that since they had a hard time winning in this world, they had better start counting heavy on the next.

SWEET RIVERS

A few more days or years at most
My troubles will be o'er,
And I shall join that heav'nly host
On Canaan's peaceful shore.
  My happy soul will drink and feast
  On love's unbounded sea;
  The glorious hope of endless rest
  Is pleasing news to me.

There are some Hallelujah songs like "When the Roll is Called Up Yonder," most of which came in as part of the camp meeting revivals, but even these are shouts of joy because of the pleasures of the expected world to come.

About eleven o'clock some of the throats tired and a lady in the altos sent her daughter up on the platform to get a sack of Christmas candy to pass out among the singers. The little girl, who was small and solemn and about four years old knew the way. I had camped by the pulpit with my tape recorder, and she had already made about thirty trips to the candy sack, each time getting just one, poking it in her mouth like a chipmunk, and very seriously handing me the cellophane wrapper to dispose of.

We sang till noon and then moved out to the long tables that were situated in a pine grove just north of the meeting house. The women had been drifting out to the tables before the singing stopped, so by the time we got there, the boxes and baskets had been unpacked and the tables were spread with food. I have as yet to go to a dinner on the grounds where there wasn't enough food to feed the multitudes four times over, but if you are a visitor the ladies all worry that you won't get your plate filled soon enough: "You better hurry yourself or they'll eat it all up from you." The tables at Harris Chapel looked about a hundred feet long, and there wasn't a bare spot on them, to start off with at least.

We ate and stood around under the pines talking till after one o'clock. Small family groups wandered through the cemetery visiting their folks who had already crossed the sweet river. They'd stop by a long-gone uncle or aunt, talk about them, and lovingly pull the weeds from the grave site. One family settled under the shade of two huge cedars near the front of the cemetery and talked easily of the business and gossip of their kin. Finally, eight or ten of the singers drifted back to the meeting house and began singing, and they all followed the sound back inside, formed the square and started again as strongly as ever before.

Somewhere around three o'clock they began to taper off, and as we got to the end everyone became more reflective and personal about the songs. The leaders dedicated songs to their parents who slept among the old folks, or would comment how much they had enjoyed the singing that day. The presiding elder took the center as the last leader. He was an old man who had more friends and kinfolks on the other side than he had here. He said, "I'll welcome you back next year if I'm still here and if your health holds." Then they all stood and sang their final hymn, "Longing for Heaven," with hope and sadness. A prayer that humbly accepted all the workings of God, good or bad, closed the singing, and the brothers of the band embraced each other and the women hugged their sisters and children, and the sense of kinship was strong.

You probably won't be able to like this music the first time around. It's too different from the First Church sound that we are accustomed to. In time, its roots go back beyond our own musical training. And an understanding and appreciation of Sacred Harp requires something that our society plays down, and that is an understanding of suffering as a natural and endurable part of life. The marketplace would have its customers believe that they can avoid suffering if they have the right kind of car or if they keep smelling good and stay slim. And if things still go wrong they can take a tranquilizer or write Abby. The Old Harper believes that suffering is as much a part of life as sundown, and the only thing that helps is to recognize it and sing about it.

CORRER DEL PAISANO

Old Man M. Tankersley of the Concho Country allowed as how there might be a mite of gold left in Californy—dang shore wasn't any left in Texas, only longhorn cattle. So he hired him a crew, throwed a herd together and pointed them for Horsehead crossing and points west.

The crew Old Man M put on, like his cattle, nearly all wore road brands. But there was a difference; Old Man M's cattle were legitimately his but these hands belonged to the law—if the law could lay hands on them.

A far-sighted fellow, Old Man M knew he'd better sell the *remuda* in California as quick as he could, save only a horse for himself and one for pack and hightail it back to Texas. The kind of fellows moving this herd wouldn't be the proper escort for a man loaded with the gold he expected to get for his cattle and horses.

Of course, now, the boys wanted to stay in Californy, but he knew them better than they knew themselves. The first night after the first payday they would blow their wages and then neither Texas nor its laws would look too bad to them, after all.

So it was. "Mr. M," their spokesman said, "we boys jist believe we'll turn around and go back to Texas with you after all."

"I'll be damned, fellers," said Old Man M, in what sounded like genuine regret. "Whyn't ye let me know sooner. Now I've done sold off the *remuther*."

Paul Patterson
Sierra Blanca, Texas

CONTRIBUTORS

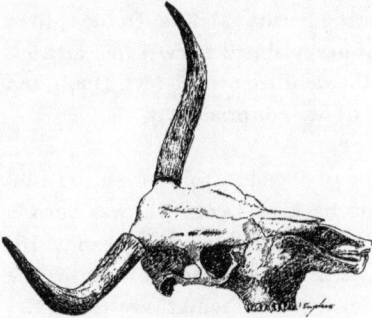

FRANCIS EDWARD ABERNETHY is a professor of English at Stephen F. Austin State University and is the Secretary-Editor of the Texas Folklore Society.

MODY C. BOATRIGHT (1896-1970) followed Dobie as Secretary-Editor of the Society and held that position from 1943 until 1963, during part of which time he was also head of The University of Texas English Department. The Society will hurt for a long time because of the loss of that dear and lovely man. Mody was of the old school and his roots were deep in the Texas soil. Ernest Speck, Mody's son-in-law, who is editing a Boatright collection, provided the present essay from Mody's papers.

BILL BRETT is the postmaster at Hull, Texas, on the southwest edge of the Big Thicket. Bill has lived a good, rich life and has drifted, cowboyed, and rodeoed through a lot of interesting times and places. He has a good ear for the idiom of his area and a good sense of story. He is a prolific writer.

J. MASON BREWER spent a long time away from Texas before he returned in 1968 to teach at East Texas State University. He was the first Negro folklorist to achieve any distinction through the Society and has published with it since 1932. "More of the Word on the Brazos" consists of tales Mason collected for his *The Word on the Brazos* (1953) but didn't use. Mason is a true soul brother.

J.FRANK DOBIE (1888-1964) was the Secretary-Editor of the Texas Folklore Society from 1923 to 1943. He infused the Society with his own strength and vitality and he remains its guardian spirit. Bertha McKee Dobie edited "Observations & Reflections" from some of her husband's newspaper articles. I hope that Dobie readers are conscious of the debt we owe to Mrs. Dobie and properly appreciate the volume and quality of her editorial work.

BILL C. MALONE is an associate professor of social history at Tulane University, but his friends are trying to get him back to Texas. Bill was born in East Texas and raised to the tune of gospel and country string bands. His *Country Music, USA* is a definitive and a classic study of an art form that he knows by heart and head. He's working on a sequel, tentatively titled *The Lingering South: Country Music in an Urban Society.*

ELTON MILES is the Director of the Division of Language Arts and Fine Arts at Sul Ross State University. He is the author of *Southwest Humorists* in the Southwest Writers Series and of several publications in the Society's journals, in addition to editing two books on Southwestern lore.

PATRICK B. MULLEN is an associate professor of English in folklore and American literature at Ohio State University. He is one of the modern breed of trained and professional folklorists, with a Ph.D. in folklore from The University of Texas. He has published widely and nationally and is deeply involved in research in applied folklore. Pat was one of my first students in folklore and I am paternally proud of him.

WILLIAM A. OWENS, born in Pin Hook, Texas, has had a full life as a university professor, novelist, and folklorist. "Return to Pin Hook" is an excerpt from his sequel to *This Stubborn Soil* and illustrates the power of the past as an inseparable part of a man's life. Bill has been teaching and writing at Columbia University since 1947 and is also the Dean of the Columbia Summer Session. Some part of him, however, is still in Texas, and the traditions of East Texas and his youth are still incubating in that part of him that creates.

LOIS WILLIAMS PARKER is a librarian at Lamar State University in Beaumont. She was born and raised in the Big Thicket and is one of the leading lights in the Big Thicket Association. Her *Big Thicket Bibliography* is the starting place for any serious study of the area.

PAUL PATTERSON of Sierra Blanca was a Pecos cowboy, hillbilly, disc jockey and rodeo announcer before he settled on teaching as a career. He taught Spanish, history, and journalism at Crane, Texas, for nearly thirty years. His stories in this volume, as well as his book *Pecos Tales,* grew out of his life in West Texas.

JOYCE GIBSON ROACH lives with Claude and two children, Darrell and Delight, near Keller, Texas. She has an M.A. from Texas Christian University and is doing graduate work at North Texas. And she burns to write. She has already published in the Society's annuals and in several popular western magazines. Joyce will be a professional.

MARTIN STAPLES SHOCKLEY, originally a Virginian, is professor of English at North Texas State University and "a Texan by choice." He's a writer of every genre and classification and a past president of all the most dignified professional societies in Texas. Martin is a gentleman of wit and discernment and we're proud that he's one of us.

R. HENDERSON SHUFFLER is Executive Director of The University of Texas Institute of Texan Cultures at San Antonio and Director of The Texana Program at The University of Texas. Henderson wrote "San Jacinto, As She Was" as a *jeu d'esprit* for a private audience several years ago. I have long enjoyed it privately and I read it to my classes when I can work it .in. He has permitted me to publish it only after long and earnest entreaties and veiled threats of revelations of certain lurid details of his past.

C. L. SONNICHSEN is presently professor of English at The University of Texas at El Paso. He has been department head, dean of the graduate school, and distinguished professor, and he claims that he's going to retire this year (1972). Leland has written fifteen books about folklore in the Southwest, which is an outstanding record when one considers that he is (or was) a Yankee. In addition to which, he makes joyful noises unto the Lord.

RONNIE C. TYLER is Curator of History at the Amon Carter Museum of Western Art in Fort Worth. He is a former professor of English, an author, and editor. Ron has done much to preserve a pictorial and artistic record of Southwestern life and traditions.

ILLUSTRATOR

JAMES R. SNYDER is an associate professor of art at Stephen F. Austin State University. He was reared in Michigan but shifted his allegiance to the West when he went to graduate school at Utah State. Since then he has shown and sold his watercolors of western life and scenes all over the United States. He raises horses and spends his summers working on a Wyoming ranch, and he looks like a young Bill Cody.

TFS HISTORY

HISTORY

The Texas Folklore Society was founded jointly by John Avery Lomax and Leonidas Warren Payne, Jr. When Lomax returned in 1907 from his year at Harvard he brought with him George Lyman Kittredge's suggestion that he establish an organization for collecting Texas folklore. Payne, who had come to The University of Texas in 1906 to teach English, was interested in folk speech. Conversations between Payne and Lomax, then teaching at Texas A&M, led to the presentation at the 1909 meeting of the Texas State Teachers Association in Dallas of a resolution to form "The Folk-Lore Society of Texas." Payne became the first president and Lomax the first secretary, and together they worked out plans and details. By April 10 they had enrolled ninety-two charter members.

Next to the American Folklore Society, the Texas Folklore Society is the oldest folklore organization still functioning in the United States. The first meeting was held on the campus of The University of Texas in 1911. Mrs. Bess Brown Lomax was on the program with a paper on the now famous "Boll Weevil" song, which Lomax had collected in the Brazos bottom in 1909. (He had returned to The University in 1910.) Kittredge attended the third meeting and gave three talks. Annual meetings have continued regularly since 1911, except for interruptions in 1918-1921 and 1944-45 caused by the great wars or their after effects. The Society has stimulated the recording and study of the rich folk culture of Texas and the Southwest, has attracted both laymen and scholars, and has distributed its publications throughout America and the world.

ANNUAL MEETINGS

The Society meets just before Easter, when members read papers on a variety of folklore subjects. On Thursday night there is a "sing" and on Friday night a dinner with an invited speaker. All sessions are open to the public. Occasionally the Society combines a meeting and an outing, as when it met in Alpine and visited the Big Bend from there.

PUBLICATIONS

In 1916 Stith Thompson, then secretary, oversaw the publication of the Society's first volume, for which Kittredge wrote the preface. This volume was entitled Publication No. I, and was reprinted in 1935 as *Round the Levee*. In 1923 J. Frank Dobie took over as secretary-treasurer, and in the following twenty years of his tenure edited an impressive collection of Texas and Mexican border lore in sixteen numbered volumes. Ever since Publication No. II was issued in 1923, the Society has sent out a book annually to its members, although some have not been numbered publications of its own.

The tradition established by J. Frank Dobie was continued by Mody C. Boatright when he assumed the office of secretary-editor in 1943. He had assisted Dobie in editing Dobie's last five volumes. Harry Ransom also participated in editing the last four. Boatright served for twenty years and produced fifteen volumes. He was succeeded by Wilson M. Hudson, who had been associate editor since 1951. In 1971 the Society's office was moved to the Stephen F. Austin State University campus in Nacogdoches, and Francis Edward Abernethy became the secretary-editor.

The volumes published by the Society contain many of the papers read at its meetings and other articles both volunteered and solicited. Most contributions are the product of original collection, and together they constitute a wealth of material in the various branches of folklore. Some topics dealt with in past publications are home remedies for man and beast, cowboy songs, Negro songs and tales, games, oil field lore, diction used in various occupations, tales of the border Mexicans, German customs, superstitions, weather signs, yarns about birds and snakes, Indian myths and legends, the origins of place-names, lore of the high plains, of the Gulf coast, of the brush country, household rhymes, and traditional songs. *Texas Folk and Folklore* (1954) is made up of items that appeared in earlier volumes. In recent publications the amount of space devoted to folklore studies as distinguished from folklore collections has increased.

MEMBERSHIP

Although the Society was originated by college teachers and has always had its office on a university campus, it is not exclusively academic in its membership. Its members are doctors, lawyers, bankers, ranchers, farmers, businessmen and housewives. Anyone may join, whether a resident of Texas or not. Libraries and other institutions belong to the Society and have continuation subscriptions to our publications.

Membership is recorded upon payment of the annual dues of $7.50, and members receive the annual publication or some other folklore book selected by the editors for distribution in the years when a book is not brought out by the Society.

This is a nonprofit organization; money received from dues pays the cost of printing or purchasing the annual volume. The small margin left over from the sale of books to nonmembers is applied to the expenses of the office.

Our emblem is the roadrunner, called *paisano* by border folk, which epitomizes the free spirit of the brush country. J. Frank Dobie chose the paisano for the Society—and for himself—years ago.

MANUSCRIPTS

Unsolicited manuscripts and art work are accepted from members only, and they cannot be returned unless they are accompanied by a self-addressed, stamped envelope. The editor will take every precaution to prevent loss of manuscripts, but no responsibility can be assumed for unsolicited materials.

Address communications to:

The Texas Folklore Society
University Station
Nacogdoches, Texas 75961

INDEX

Typesetting / LUCAS & CLARK TYPESETTING

Paper / FINE PAPER COMPANY

Printing / CAPITAL PRINTING COMPANY

Binding / CUSTOM BOOKBINDERS

Design / WILLIAM D. WITTLIFF

www.ingramcontent.com/pod-product-compliance
Lightning Source LLC
Chambersburg PA
CBHW021829020426
42334CB00014B/556